William George Thorpe

The hidden Lives of Shakespeare and Bacon and their Business Connection

With some Revelations of Shakespeare's early Struggles, 1587-1592

William George Thorpe

The hidden Lives of Shakespeare and Bacon and their Business Connection
With some Revelations of Shakespeare's early Struggles, 1587-1592

ISBN/EAN: 9783337081218

Printed in Europe, USA, Canada, Australia, Japan

Cover: Foto ©ninafisch / pixelio.de

More available books at **www.hansebooks.com**

THE HIDDEN LIVES OF SHAKESPEARE AND BACON

AND THEIR BUSINESS CONNECTION;

WITH SOME REVELATIONS OF SHAKESPEARE'S EARLY STRUGGLES 1587-1592.

BY

W. G. THORPE, F.S.A.

OF THE MIDDLE TEMPLE.

AUTHOR OF "THE STILL LIFE OF THE MIDDLE TEMPLE,"
"MIDDLE TEMPLE TABLE TALK," ETC.

"Tot ou Tard, tout se sçait."

LONDON:
PRINTED FOR THE AUTHOR AT THE CHISWICK PRESS
1897

[All rights reserved.]

I

INSCRIBE THIS BOOK TO

THOMAS WILLIAM BROOKES

of the Convent, Kingsgate, Thanet, in remembrance of nearly forty years' friendship and esteem.

But I must, in common gratitude, record thus publicly the sympathy, aid, and encouragement accorded me in this novel and difficult inquiry by

SAM. TIMMINS, J.P., F.S.A.,

of Spring Hill, Arley, Coventry, the widely known scholar and student of Shakespeare, to whose literature he has for over forty years devoted all the powers of his mind, and in whose "The Shakespeare Year" the world of the Poet's admirers yearly find a careful and thoroughly reliable account of all that has occurred to interest them in the previous period.

TO THE READER.

Mr. Halliwell-Phillipps in his "Outlines of the Life of Shakespeare," seventh edition, thus forecasts the future of the still expanding Shakespeare cult.

"IN the absence of some very important and unexpected discovery, the general desire to penetrate the mystery which surrounds the personal history of Shakespeare cannot be gratified.

"It is not likely that much beyond a very imperfect sketch of the material features of his life will ever be revealed . . . but so vivid is the general interest enforced by the publication of the minutest new fact regarding the world's greatest author that this unsatisfactory position hardly accounts for an inclination not unfrequently manifested . . . for the setting up of a mythical Shakespeare.

"Such an inclination may sometimes arise from a reluctance to believe that the object of our idolatry could ever have been human.

"It is a delusion that Shakespeare's transcendent intellect excluded the admission of human frailty."

Thus prophesied the man who has done the most to clear up the mystery! and had he lived to see the revelation of the "important and unexpected discovery" he saw afar off, he would have found his prediction verified, even had it been his own lot to proclaim to the world, the secret which lay all the while *easily within his reach.*

Hardly, even for him, would publishers have dared to face the (possible, even now) howl of execration awaiting the man who might assert that Shakespeare was not nursed by fairies and cradled in violets, was not lawyer, statesman, linguist, and scientist combined.

In fact, they are equally timorous now, and but for my reliance on the evidence hereafter adduced, and my faith that Truth must prevail in the end, I should not have put forward and challenged criticism on the following astounding propositions, which, however, the chief authority at Stratford-on-Avon has stamped with his approval—the MS. being printed exactly as it left that gentleman's hands. In his own words to me, it fits exactly together, and cannot be got out of; with him, at all events, the Truth is above all sentimental and preconceived considerations of however long standing. In such a spirit, gentle reader, I ask you to approach the following positions, which directly arise from the book in your hands.

(1.) That Shakespeare, at all events up to 1599, kept a gold, silver, and "copper" hell, carrying on this last in the open streets with yokels, and putting on workman's dress in order to appear to be on their level and thus more easily gain their confidence.

(2.) That by this means he supplied the wants of his "hungry famylee" (one of Mr. Halliwell's standing puzzles).

(3.) That he purchased New Place out of the money got by rooking an infant young gentleman : these circumstances being matter of notoriety among his townsmen and neighbours, gentle and simple.

Now take another tack.

A. That deer-stealing was felony punishable in the Star Chamber, for which Bacon (practically the Public Prosecutor until he became Chancellor) prosecuted two men separately as late as 1614.

B. That hence, if an information was laid, it was in Bacon's power to have dealt similarly with Shakespeare any time between the date of the offence in 1587 and the 1614 aforesaid.

C. That if Bacon did not so prosecute, but rather protected him, there must have been good (Baconian) reason for it. Now Bacon blackmailed everybody, and hunted his patron Essex to the death for money.

D. Thirteen years after his Hegira from Stratford, Shakespeare's offence was remembered and cast up against him. He had fled for very fear. Can this be the reason why he did not revisit his native town for ten years, and then only for his son's funeral, when pity might stay the hand of the avenger? Can this, too, be the cause why he "lay low" and kept out of sight in London, lived in a Bankside lodging, and did not ruffle it bravely as did Henslow, Alleyne, and Burbage, actor-managers like himself? Here are two more of the conundrums Mr. Halliwell despaired of solving.

E. Shakespeare was completely in Bacon's power, by the double ties of profitable employment flowing inwards, and the fear of the terrors of the law which stood ready at Bacon's hand. We know that Bacon cadged for the smallest item of "copy" for the Twickenham Scrivenery, so that Shakespeare's theatre-writing would not pass overlooked.

And yet, as often happens, the victim had (perhaps from some hold springing out of Bacon's private life) a back pull which enabled him to constrain his master to put off another pressing creditor (as we know he did), and pay him out of Catesby's fine, really the blood-money for which he had sold Essex, the amount which paid for the Combe Estate; yet one more point which puzzled Mr. Halliwell as he plaintively confesses.

It may be, gentle reader—I trust, indeed, it is—that this investigation which I have had the happy chance to open, may, if followed up by abler hands, throw more light still on this hitherto unworked inquiry. I do but ask you to be not shocked by the announcement, but courageously compare, side by side, the baseless theory of a glorified superhuman Shakespeare with the hard facts which I endeavour in this book to oppose to it.

I make Shakespeare neither better nor worse than any other man. I bow before, and acknowledge, his marvellous talents and gifts. I in no way impeach the authorship of his works—I but show the man as he was, hardly tried, with all possible means of earning his living denied him, yet doing his best, and a desperate best, too, to keep the wolf from the door of those whom he loved, and whose daily bread he must, at all hazards, provide.

W. G. THORPE.

GLOUCESTER HOUSE,
    LARKHALL RISE, S.W.
        New Year's Eve, 1896.

TABLE OF CONTENTS.

	PAGE
INTRODUCTION	xix

CHAPTER I.

The Immortality of Poets—Envied by Heroes—Wolfe and Gray's "Elegy"—Public Interest in great Poets' Lives—Cryprograms useless for such purposes—Parallel Passages only tantalizing—Shakespeare's personal Surroundings hunted up Microscopically—Now exhausted—Bacon's Life recorded voluminously—The two Biographies never compared for possible Points of Contact—Yet Bacon directed the Gray's Inn Masque of 1594, Mounted by the Chamberlain's Players, of which Shakespeare Factotum Manager—The two in Hand-grip then, if not before, and continuing so till Shakespeare died—Ben Jonson a Common Friend—Present when Shakespeare got his Death and Apologist for Bacon in his Degradation—"O rare Ben Jonson"—Origin of Present Inquiry—The writer's Copy of First Folio 1623—The Second-Hand Book Catalogue—The MS. Pamphlet the "Apologie" 1600—Bacon's Allusion to his Public Scrivenery at Twickenham—Publication of facts in "The Academy" of March 30th and April 13th, 1895—The "Apologie" a Key to all that follows the proximate cause of Essex's Death and Forfeiture—And a Clue to the Five Dark Years of Shakespeare's Life, 1587-92 1

CHAPTER II.

Elizabethan Society thoroughly corrupt—The Queen's Intimacy with Essex, and her Jealousy of him—She drives Maids of Honour from Court with blows and curses—Essex's Liaison with Lady Rutland brings about Elizabeth's Signature to his Death Warrant—Allen, Faunt, and Standen upon Court Morals—Lord Keeper makes over the sale of Pardons to the Court Ladies, to eke out their stipends—Bacon appears as a Broker herein—Terrible Gambling among all ranks—Northbrooke's evidence 1577—Gambling in Inns of Court Halls—Cause of the Bacon Brothers' ruin—Bacon comes from Paris to London 1597—Master of Revels at Gray's Inn 1588—Directs Plays and Masques before the Queen and his uncle, Lord Burleigh—Who will not employ him in Government Service on account of his Follies and Vices—Shakespeare has to leave Stratford in 1587 on account of a "Star Chamber" offence and slips away in the train of the Players—The Company Prosper, and oust all Competitors, finally appearing at Court where (if not earlier) he would meet Bacon—It mounts the Gray's Inn Masque of 1588 before the Court—Bacon meets Essex in 1591 and obtains complete Influence over him—Essex's Bravery still recorded on the Walls of Cadiz—Bacon introduces his brother Anthony as Essex's Foreign Secretary—Scrivenery set up at Twickenham Park for the Correspondence—By Standen's order the Cipher never intrusted to Essex—Bacon's Mother, Lady Ann—Her close watch upon her Sons and her absolute Tyranny over them—Her Complaints that Bacon's Gambling had led to his "early discredit" (*i.e.*, loss of Character), and of the Drunken Habits of both Brothers—She spent her whole Substance upon them, and was Bacon's sole Money Resource—Shakespeare's Position in 1594—How did he Subsist and keep his Family from 1587?—All Biographers at fault here—The only possible Solution Winnings at Play—Parallels in the Lives of Crockford and Swindell—No Personal Disgrace in all three cases—The Great Duke of Wellington asking to be Elected

to Crocky's—Cutting Double or Quits for £90,000
—But this solution of Shakespeare's Rise provable by direct Contemporary Evidence—Sir John
Harrington—His Character by the present Bishop
of London—His knowledge of Gaming—His
"Nugæ Antiquæ" written 1597—Three Extracts
from it—At this time Shakespeare buys "New
Place"—Sir John a frequent Resident at Combe
Abbey close by, and the talk there as to where the
Purchase Money came from—Incidental Proof that
Shakespeare was a man not to be trifled with—
Strange Infrequency of References to Gambling in
Shakespeare's Plays, even Disapproval of it in
Hamlet—Why? 8

CHAPTER III.

About 1590 Theatres under a Cloud—In 1594 Gray's
Inn decide upon a Play and Pageant—Their Plays
usually Classical Translations by one of themselves—Any such Translation, if not written by an
Accomplished Latinist like Bacon, would be Revised
by him as Master of the Revels—The Masque contained six Speeches by Bacon and one Song by
Campion—Who contributed the "Last Songe?"—
Who Contributed the "Dancing Songe?" Who
read up Gilbert's Latin "De Magnete" and wrote
the Discussions on Magnetism?—Rehearsals at
Gray's Inn—The Bolt from the Blue—Lady Ann
Bacon—Will she attend the Performance and
thoroughly Purge the Pit—Similar Maestingers—
Sarah Lady Jersey, Mrs. "Diamond" Hope, etc.—
How Lady Ann Rebuked Essex, her sons' Patron, for
Adultery, and how Meekly he took it—The Bacons
cannot offend their only Friend—The Performance
must come off, but Authorship can be shifted on to
Stage Manager, to whom the Play stuck—Why
called "Errors"—Intimacy quietly continued between Bacon and Shakespeare until Lady Ann's

Death, when Bacon Solicitor-General—Bacon gets up Masque for the Palatine's Wedding and offers to do so for Carre's—His letter to Carre—Evidence of Sodality with Players—How close Mr. Spedding came to finding out the Secret Link 27

CHAPTER IV.

The Scrivenery—Anthony Burleigh's "Foreign Intelligencer" on the Continent for some years—Return to England 1592—Sets up a Scrivenery for Copying Manuscripts for sale—Slighted by the Cecils, attaches himself to their rival Esssex as Foreign Secretary—Renews connection with his old Correspondents involving much Pen work, Decipherment, and Translation—Anthony's Salary £1000 a year, £7000 now—Scrivenery removed to Twickenham Park, out of reach of the City Company's Sphere of Prohibition—Names of some of the Foreign Agents, Standen, Sir Thomas Bodley (of the Library), Guicciardini, etc.—Treachery on every side—How Essex was able to provide for this Enormous Expense—His Gifts from the Queen alone averaging £210,000 a year (of our money) besides his Places, £35,000 more—Anthony blackmails Essex out of Essex House, only leaving it afterwards by the Queen's Special Order—Mentions of the Scrivenery in History—Standen—Colman—James, the Cadiz Relation—The "Apologie"—Topcliffe and, after Anthony's Death, Dorset—The Theatre Work done for Shakespeare was the only way by which the Dramatist could get repaid the loans which he could not refuse making to Bacon as Master of Gray's Inn Revels—From a Letter to Lord Shrewsbury, asking the loan of a "Horse and Armour" for some public show, Bacon seems to have Directed Public Pageants—Twickenham would provide Amanuenses to write down the Plays—Would copy out the MSS. without a blot, and supply Prompters' parts and Actors' lengths as and when required—Moreover, as it would not do to run about to several places, all the acting Plays would be kept at Twickenham 40

CHAPTER V.

Burleigh in 1598 wishes peace with Spain; Essex Opposes it, and Appeals to the Nation in a Pamphlet styled the "Apologie" sent out from Twickenham broadcast, like the Cadiz Relation—The Queen resents it bitterly—He Insults her, she boxes his ears and goes off in a Huff—Quarrel patched up, but from this time dates Essex's Fall—Liége spy reports to Cecil that Foreigners accuse the Bacons of making the King of Spain Ridiculous on the Stage as if they Controlled a Theatre (a Statement subsequently confirmed by Essex)—Essex Intrigues again with Maids of Honour whom Elizabeth drives from Court with Blows and Curses—In September, 1599, Essex Imprisoned in his own house under a Keeper for eight months—Nearly Dying in the Time—His Monopoly of Sweet Wines taken from him by the Crown—The Bacons in sore Money Straits also—Francis implores the Queen for a Grant of Land, "Creditors are Suing him and Insulting him"—Anthony Blackmails Essex and gets all he had left—Essex House, Strand—Elizabeth furious and forces the Family to Redeem it—Bacon sees no more is to be gained by Essex's Life, but if (as Elizabeth's Custom was) the Forfeiture consequent on his Attainder and Death enured to the man who brought it about, there was great Profit in view—The Plan commenced—Lady Rich's Unhappy Letter—As Elizabeth had been Provoked by "The Apologie"—Bacon prints it together with this last and circulates it by Anthony's servants, *i.e.*, his own (*Vide* his own words, Abbott, Bacon and Essex, App. p. 1.)—Elizabeth Furious—Imprisons two men and tries to get in all the Copies—Two Contemporary

Letters from Sydney Papers—Essex in Despair—He also seeks to stop Circulation; ultimately effects it—He writes the Queen that those who had thrown him aside like a dead Carcase had Printed him and would Play him on the Stage—Implying the Bacons control of a Theatre—Essex is Executed—Anthony Dies of Remorse within four months—Destroying his later Correspondence—In the Autumn Bacon receives some of Essex's Blood-Money—But Shakespeare receives most of it and Purchases in the following Spring the Combe Lands—Halliwell's query as to where this money came from, Answered—On Shakespeare's Death, Ben Jonson applies to Lord Chancellor Bacon for a Subscription to a Monument—He receives back an Epitaph—

"What needs my Shakespeare for his hallowed bones?"

Why this was Omitted from the First Folio of 1623 and only published anonymously in the Second Folio of 1632—The two wholly different men United in Bacon—MISERERE DOMINE 51

APPENDIX 67

INDEX 77

INTRODUCTION.

THIS book has nothing in common with the so-called Bacon-Shakespeare controversy, nor does it seek to impugn the accepted authorship of the plays. Its object is merely to prove from contemporary evidence, from papers under Bacon's hand and the logic of facts, the existence for over twenty years of a close intimacy between poet and philosopher, involving large business transactions both in theatrical and monetary matters.

The evidence will, in every instance, be set out in the text.

The investigation, of which these pages are the outcome, sprung from my casually perusing a document in Spedding's exhaustive life of Bacon. It is undated and unaddressed, but the learned editor fixes it as written in 1613, and addressed to Carre, the favourite of James I., with which period alone in Bacon's life can it possibly interleave.

The original can be seen among the Bacon MSS. in Lambeth Palace Library, and it opens out to us from the outset a very peculiar and hitherto unsuspected story; for, firstly, it is one of the greatest rarities in the great philosopher's life, A DRAFT in his own handwriting. We know that he wrote out his works seven times over, but I can only call to mind the existence of two drafts; this, and the Comentarius Solutus—a private note-book of his plans and means, which is printed at length in Spedding, "Life," vol. iv., p. 40. But that a draft of this letter should exist seems to prove that the document itself required much consideration before its despatch, and that, too, from one of the most cautious and secretive of mankind. Secondly, it is the one and only admission by the great philosopher under his own hand of his connection and personal intimacy with the Lord Chamberlain's Company of Players, of which Shakespeare was Actor-Manager-factotum. "Gray's Inn was much bounden to them"—the actors are almost treated as equals, if not more.

Of course there already existed circumstances, which I had the good fortune to bring out two years ago, and in which the logic of facts left no escape from these two conclusions.

(1.) That in 1594, if not previously, Bacon, as Master of Gray's Inn Revels, had employed this company to mount a masque, and perform a play in that society's hall, involving thereby the three important relations of employer and employed, critic and stage-manager, paymaster and payee.

Bacon would be keen on making the pageant a success, and be present at most of the rehearsals, which extended over three weeks.

(2.) That these relations went on without check

or hitch for twenty years, up to 1614, when Bacon "devised" the sumptuous masque and water pageant for the Elector Palatine's marriage with the king's daughter Elizabeth. Shortly afterwards he again employed this same company to perform a masque at a cost to himself of £2,000, say £14,000 of our money.

This letter shows that he held the players in personal esteem, but that is by no means all, for it is the one remnant left to us (and that assuredly by a slip) of the voluminous theatrical correspondence (not to speak of accounts and receipts for money paid), to which Bacon was a party, during this double decade. The Elizabethan was a letter-writing age, and people for the most part preserved their correspondence, unless there came to be a risk in keeping it, when they promptly put it out of reach of a Privy Council Warrant, and its search officer.

For some such cause Anthony Bacon must have destroyed the concluding portion of his papers, and for an equally good reason his brother Francis made away with his stage correspondence. He was good at suppressing awkward matters, such as the nature of his wife's misconduct, and his scrivenery business; of which, oddly enough, the only record under his hand also exists in the Lambeth Palace collection. Yet he kept it going till 1609, and even *touted* for work for it, though then a rich man.

Some one seems to have hinted this last to Mr. Spedding, but he brushed the suggestion aside Yet, had he coupled it with the letter to Anthony in 1594, on which he never comments at all, he would have been very near the discovery which, in abler hands than mine, may yet have more to tell us.

So great was Bacon's ascendancy over the minds of men, that those who knew both secrets, the stage and the Scrivenery, dared only refer to it with bated breath. The *Liége* spy wrote it to the Cecils, but they kept it dark; even the unhappy Essex, when denouncing the Bacons as his betrayers, dared say no more than "they play me on the stage and now they print me." The Queen knew well enough whom he alluded to.

There is a touch of sadness in looking at my own MS. copy of this so "printed" item, the "Apologie." It was written by Essex's request at the Scrivenery, for his private use, and the fact of such request, may, a few days later, have suggested to the Bacons what a terrible power the "printing" would have to effect his ruin. Essex taunted Bacon with this on his trial. It had been the first cause of his decline in the Queen's favour three years before: Elizabeth never forgave it, and Chamberlain tells us of the spasm of fury which seized her when it was "printed" as Bacon tells us, by himself, practically. It was the death-warrant of the high-souled Englishman, on whose gallant memory rests none of the treachery in which Elizabeth's courtiers were for the most part adepts.

But it occurred to me that, in a life lived so much in public as was Bacon's, there must be points at which these secrets would work up close to the surface, so that anyone on the lookout might verify their existence; just as the Esquimaux waits at a seal's blow-hole on the ice till the animal comes up to breathe; and with this view I read through Bacon's acted life as disclosed in facts.

But I also kept in view the few leading occurrences in Shakespeare's life, so as to lay hold of any possible points of contact.

I was thus in a position to synchronize Bacon's receipt of money with Shakespeare's large purchase of land at about the same amount, and, above all, when turning over Harrington, to detect the long overlooked references, and verify them by the local surroundings at Combe Abbey. As in my discovery of the warrant for Bunyan's arrest for that imprisonment during which he wrote "Pilgrim's Progress," the wonder is how it has been so overlooked! To speak of only a few, it has escaped Halliwell, Collier, Mr. Fleay, Dr. Furnivall, and Dr. Mandell Creighton, the present Bishop of London, who wrote the life of Harrington in the "Dictionary of National Biography."

It is plain, also, from Mr. Park's preface to his 1804 edition of "Nugæ Antiquæ," that his pages were gone through, and his notes corrected by so keen a Shakespearian as Malone, as also the Antiquaries Bindley and Douce, who, with so keen a critic as Professor Porson, followed Malone's lead in failing to detect the thinly-veiled secret, which it is my happiness now to bring to light.

My discovery of the Bacon-Shakespeare connection was announced in my "Middle Temple Table Talk," in 1894—"The Academy" of March 3rd and April 14th, 1895, published the account of the "Scrivenery," and invited students' attention to a possibly new field of research; some of them told me they had looked over it but did not see their way to contradict or challenge: "there was something staggering about it." I print these as an appendix.

On the contrary, Mr. Sam. Timmins, F.S.A., wrote, accepting my conclusions unreservedly, and asked for any further information to be incorporated in his Annual Review of things Shakespearian—"The Shakespeare Year"—a kind of Annual Register of the cult. I was luckily at the moment in a position to enable him to foreshadow the (then not thoroughly worked out) Harrington revelation.

When, however, the local fillings in were completed, I placed the MS. in Mr. Timmins's hands for perusal and verification. He honoured it with unqualified approval, suggesting some alterations which were at once accepted. The book now appears as it left his hands, and I hope he will pardon my saying that I could not have placed it before any better qualified authority.

Henceforth, if I am right, the lives of Shakespeare and Bacon are inseparably connected in three respects: personal intimacy, theatrical pursuits, and money matters. I foresee at least one more to come. One rejoices, however, to think that, in the dark shadows which gloom over so much of the great philosopher's life, the great poet has no share. On the contrary, in that one especial stain, the judicial murder of their common friend and patron, Essex, Shakespeare's dumb protest stands clearly on record.

Bacon, as we know, was one of the most thin-skinned of mortals, and, after the deed was done, published his own "Apology" with a view of escaping some of the public opprobrium then largely being heaped on him. In other words he "PRINTED" Essex. Now gladly would he have "PLAYED HIM ON THE STAGE." But there he met with resistance —there the mighty spell of his influence failed

The Players' sympathy with the victim, which caused them to lie long under serious suspicion of complicity with his outbreak, might have been overcome, but the actor-manager stood firm. We know so little of Shakespeare's life, but here, at least, is unmistakable evidence of that high-minded principle, rightly termed a passion for truth — "Facta non verba."

The life of that great dramatist may have to be partly re-written, and I can only hope that some one with better qualifications than myself, but with equally good fortune, may discover other points of contact.

For he will have at least these grounds to go upon, that in these latter days of ours, as in those gone by, knowledge comes to him who waits, and that "there is nothing hidden which shall not be revealed."

W. G. THORPE.

THE HIDDEN LIVES OF SHAKESPEARE AND BACON.

CHAPTER I.

I SIT down to write the story of the connection which for nearly a quarter of a century united the private lives of the two most illustrious men in poetry and philosophy who ever lived—sharers in that unique and ever-green immortality confined alone to those who appeal to the minds of men.

Great conquerors are remembered in a way—Alexander's name can never wholly die, but his victories and successes are memories without present interest; while the deathless ring of Homeric cadences, even veiled in translation, still touch and stir the hearts of thousands, and will do so for all time.

Trumpet and drum sound once for all: but he who can

> "Sing of what the world shall be
> When the years have passed away"

has a voice audible throughout the ages.

The heroes themselves admit it; did not Wolfe, on the eve of his deathless victory, his the one voice audible in that silent flotilla, charm away the anxieties of that terrible dumb night-watch by repeating to those around him Gray's "Elegy"? and then continue: "Now, gentlemen, I'd rather have written that poem than take Quebec."

The hero dies as did Wolfe at the next sunrise, and his work blurs out; the poet lives—thus it is that the two great luminaries who blazed out in the Elizabethan age have an ever increasing attraction, and the apparently unslakable thirst for a solution of the problems which surround their private lives grows rather than diminishes. The inquiry has taken all manner of forms, of which the "cryptogram craze" is probably the most futile.

A cryptogram is a private mark put on an article of no present value, to evidence ownership at a future period, when something is to be gained by the assertion of proprietorship. Shakespeare's plays were of such little current value that their author never cared to collect them together in his life, and, while making bequests to their subsequent editors in his will, never intrusted the plays to those who best knew what, if anything, could be made of them. Nay, when the First Folio did appear, its editors were uneasy about its being a pecuniary success.

Hence "discovery by cryptogram" was a false issue from the first, and the "parallel passages" inquiry can never have more than a possibility as their result.

But Shakespeare's surroundings, his relatives

and their connections, where they lived, what they said and did, and every transaction in which the poor peasants were engaged are another matter; and these have been hunted up with an almost German patience, which has thrown, however, little or no light on the grand questions of "the Genesis of the Plays, their MSS., and what became of them" —for the earliest now existing is of Commonwealth age. Even this source has been gradually drying up, and it is safe to say that no new light can be thrown on Shakespeare's life from Shakespeare's side.

Yet all this while there lay hidden another mine of research, abounding in documents, and itself a part of the History of England, which surely might, at all events, be worth looking through, on the off chance of something turning up in it! But as neither Chamberlain's nor the Sydney letters mention Shakespeare, it was taken for granted that the actor was "out of Society"—as he undoubtedly was of a certain sort—and that he and Bacon never knew each other, and still less came into constant contact in business matters. Yet both Mr. Halliwell and Mr. Fleay knew that Bacon had directed the "dumb show" at the Royal Palace at Greenwich, had written an essay specially on pageants, and knew that his tastes lay strongly toward the stage. Both knew that, as an especial favourite of the Queen, he was constantly at Court, where the Lord Chamberlain's players, to which company Shakespeare was always attached, had ousted all rivals. Both knew that Bacon, as Master of the Revels at Gray's Inn in 1594, had directed the great Masque which the players, of whom Shakespeare was "factotum" manager, had mounted and put on the stage.

How could the Master of the Revels, himself a director of the "dumb show" six years back, avoid constant touch with the manager, a man whose skill in "staging" had converted a ghastly failure like Ben Jonson's "Every Man in His Humour" into a comedy which is performed even now? And how could all the commentators have missed this simple point?—how our American cousins could have overlooked it is a blindness for which one cannot account in such men.

For, in addition, there was Bacon's intimacy with Ben Jonson, a worthy fellow never in the best of feather as Henslow, Alleyne, and Burbage were, but yet an honoured guest at York Place on the Chancellor's "proudest day of his life."

He wrote an ode for this triumphal occasion, but he also, in the dark day of disgrace and humiliation then waiting at the door, loyally stood up and said what little could be said for the great man fallen so low. In an age of such unspeakable depravity and moral degradation as we shall be compelled to consider hereafter, such a refreshing interlude of kindly feeling might have recalled itself, twenty years or so later, to the bystander who caused to be cut on his grave, "O rare Ben Jonson."

> "Bright things can never die,
> E'en though they fade,"

nor, in this case at least,—a kindly heart.

But how came about the change? How is it that a new field has opened for Shakespearian research which has already developed some startling results, made it necessary for the life of Shakespeare to be re-written, and has opened a field for inquiry which may possibly, so vast is its ground, develop a library of literature only second to that already in our hands, and of which the end is not yet?

It came by apparent accident; or, rather, in Pope's words:

> "All chance, direction—which thou canst not see."

The writer possesses a First Folio of Shakespeare, and had long fretted under the little information then on record as to its author; but he did not care for the flood of rhapsodical and irrelevant matter poured then — and now — from the press, while the cryptogram was, as we have seen, inherently abhorrent.

Seeing in a bookseller's catalogue the name of a manuscript which hereafter plays a great part in unravelling the mystery, I purchased it, and submitted it to some valued friends at the British Museum and Record Office, who had greatly helped me in my discovery of the Bunyan Warrant in 1887. They gave me cold comfort. "It was a common political pamphlet of the period—it had been printed in 1603, and they had five copies, one of them in French." (These last turned out to be all somewhat rough transcripts, and ran down to 1620.)

The case looked so hopeless that, in spite of a clear individuality about the beautifully written book, the purchaser decided to ask the vendor to take it back at half-price ; but before doing so he did what, unhappily, few students do—he looked it up, there flashing across his mind the recollection that Bacon had written a letter to his brother Anthony, in which he asked him to tout for custom for an evidently extensive scrivenery carried on by him at Twickenham Park (Spedding, Life, i. 349).

The quest yielded fruit at once, and I published in "The Academy" of April 13th, 1895, a description of this "Apologie," setting out conclusions to which it pointed, inviting comments and information generally. None, however, appeared—though I was told many sat down to confute it, one of whom (a scholar far above me) abandoned the attempt, "there was something staggering about it." These letters are printed in the Appendix.

Further search brought up further and suggestive evidence, and this special MS. is now submitted to the Shakespearian world as having thrown a new light, by a hitherto untrodden path, upon the hidden life of the dramatist. When abler hands than mine take it up, " the end may not be yet " by a long way.

As it is, this pamphlet will be attempted to be shown as the instrument by which Bacon, when all chance of continuing to profit by sponging on Essex's *life* was at an end, and the only benefit open to the ruined and penniless spendthrift was through his *death, attainder,* and *forfeiture,* brought about the outbreak for which the gallant Englishman was brought to axe and block. The other evidence is from extracts from the letters of the two Bacons, their mother and their uncle, while the clinchers shall come from two distinct and independent sources, quite unknown to each other, one an English Government spy at Liége, and the other the wailing outcry in his agony of the gallant, high-minded Essex — against whom stand on record many faults and errors, but none of the despicable and ignoble meannesses which stamped all the foremost men of the age, as we shall have pitifully to note in the next chapter.

In fact, his share of the sack of Faro was the Bishop's Library, now, by his gift to his friend the illustrious founder of it, a part of the Bodleian Library.

Finally, an attempt will be made, from a hitherto unnoticed source, to clear up the mystery which shrouds the five absolutely dark years of Shakespeare's life—1587-92.

CHAPTER II.

BEFORE bringing our several performers on the scene, a few words must be said on the conditions of Society towards the end of the reign of Elizabeth, and the strong factors by which therefore all their characters were moulded.

It is hardly possible to imagine any period worse, in a moral point of view. Intrigue and profligacy were almost its sole constituents. The Queen set a most deplorable example. Lord Essex, on his return from Ireland, went splashed, and in his riding boots, straight up to her bedchamber, as if he were her husband, none staying his way. Elizabeth, with "hair about her face just as she was risen," in no way resented the intrusion, but chatted pleasantly with the newcomer!—on the contrary her jealousy of him was extreme; when he was "carrying on" with four of her maids of honour, she could drive two of them from Court with oaths and blows; and his intimacy with Lady Rutland is said by Birch (Queen Elizabeth, i. 354), to have finally forced from her the warrant for his death.

One or two proofs are permissible. When Anthony Bacon was on the point of returning to

England, Allen writes him on Aug. 17th, 1589: "There never was in Court such emulation, envy, and backbiting as is now. At the time you come home, you must

> Cogg, lie, flatter and face
> Four waies in Court to win you grace."

Faunt, Walsingham's secretary, writes to Anthony: "In Court where sin reigneth in the highest degree." Standen, chief spy first to Burleigh, then to Essex, writes him: "All Charity is exiled from Court and all envy and treachery doth prevail."

The Queen kept her bedchamber women on such scanty pay, that they had to eke out their salaries by selling pardons; in fact, the Lord Keeper, as did Jeffreys later on with the Maids of Taunton, had made over to them that department as a source of income, and we find Bacon—to whom the smallest sum of money (as we shall sorrowfully find hereafter) was irresistible—acted as a broker in the business; Standen writing him in December, 1595, that Lady Edmondes thought the £100 he had offered for a pardon was too little.

But the most shocking feature of the age was the universal gambling of all classes—apparently more widely spread than in "The early days of Charles James Fox," of whom we read in the pleasant pages of Sir George Trevelyan, who speaks of "Gambling in all its forms as rather a profession than an occupation among leaders of London Society."

A book by one Northbrooke, in 1577, called "Dicing, Drinking, Play and Interludes," tells us on p. 8:

"If a man will not dice and play, then he is a niggard and a miser and no good fellow.

"What is a man now a dayes if he know not fashion, and how to wear his apparel after the best fashion? to kepe company and to become mummer and dicer and to play their twenty, fifty or even one hundred *li* (*i.e.* pounds) at cards, dice, post, gleek, or such other games? And by such kinds of playes manie of them are brought into great miserie and penurie."

We learn from Ben Jonson that the costermongers' games were mumchance and tray trap.[1]

The unlearned, and learned classes also, had no other diversion than what is now euphoniously called the three W's. After meals taken in hall, barristers passed their time away with wine, cards, and dice. When the floor of our Middle Temple Hall (co-æval with that at Gray's Inn) was taken up, any quantity of these last, mostly cogged, were picked up which had fallen through the joints, as wide apart as those still to be seen at the historic "Cheshire Cheese" in Fleet Street.

This vice of gambling will exhibit its results

---

[1] Mumchance was played in silence; in tray trap they won throwing a trois.

prominently in our narrative for it was certainly the cause of Bacon's ruin, and if the evidence we shall adduce be accepted, of Shakespeare's rise.

Into this seething sea of corruption Bacon entered in 1579. He had graduated in vice for three years in Paris, then, and for two centuries to come, possessing the distinction now held by Tunis, of "the wickedest place on earth." Sir George Trevelyan quotes from Lord John Russell a sickening story of Fox's initiation into vice there by his own father, the first Lord Holland—let us add, however, that on the lad's return to Eton, the moral infamy which he started there brought about the youngster's prompt expulsion.

Bacon, son of a Lord Keeper, and nephew of the Prime Minister, soon became an Ancient of Gray's Inn, and some few traditions of what was called "Waterfordism" in the forties, show that he went the pace pretty much like the rest. He evidently took part in the amusements that were going, and directed a pageant played before Lord Burleigh, and a queer kind of comedy on June 16th, 1588. The next year he wrote to his uncle offering to produce another one, so he would then be officially Master of the Revels, as which he remained till 1614, twenty-six years.

On May 28th, 1588, we find Bacon acting "dumb show" in a play performed before Elizabeth by the gentlemen of Gray's Inn. We thus find Bacon actor in and director of Plays and Masques before the Queen, and his uncle Lord Burleigh, who evidently disliked what he called his nephew's "vanities" (otherwise follies and vices), declining to push him forward in the Government Service on the ground of what we should now call his "unsteadiness," which must have been very noticeable indeed, to have barred his advancement in those days. A century later, debt and dissoluteness did not delay the upward career of the infamous Jeffreys, nor, a century later still, that of Charles James Fox, or the Earl of Sandwich— nay, the Prime Minister could take a mistress picked from off the streets, and place her by his side opposite the royal box where George III. and Queen Charlotte sat in state, and afterwards wait on his Sovereign, as though nothing had happened!

Now in 1586 Shakespeare, then affected with the same complaint, had got into a serious scrape at Stratford for deer-stealing; there must have been something remarkable about this business, for as we shall see, it stuck to him in after years. However, he had to slip away in the train of a London theatre company, then on tour there. That company eventually prospered, and after many changes of name, became known as the Lord Chamberlain's Players, by which name it will be styled in these pages. It lasted till 1641, when for twenty years theatres were to cease to exist. By good management, suitable wardrobe and plant, it ousted all its competitors from the

Court, and performed there on six recorded occasions in the winter of 1591-2. These were at Whitehall, and there were others in the following winter.

As the Gray's Inn Masque of 1588 before the Court would require some kind of mounting, dresses, rehearsals, and drilling for the dumb shows in which Bacon acted, there must have been some kind of what we call professional assistance derived from the actors; we therefore may fairly refer the acquaintance of Bacon with Shakespeare to that date at all events, though it is hard to conceive the racketty young barrister not going to all the theatres, and knowing all the actors, especially one pushing young man among them who did all round good service, and managed to make money in a way we shall unhappily describe later on. But from December 27th, 1591, their acquaintance is unavoidable. It must have improved too, under the added accessories of drink and the dice box, for before the year was out the two were to be in co-operation and intimate hand-grip for twenty-two years. Money changed hands on that occasion, if not before, and was to continue doing so till Bacon paid the actor £2,000 out of his own money to perform a mask at the latter date.

In 1591 Bacon formed the acquaintance of Robert Devereux, second Earl of Essex, over whom he at once exercised great influence; upon whom he lived for certainly the nine following years; and whom, if popular report, and the story we have to tell be true, he betrayed to the death, when his patron's ruin was so complete that he could no longer make a profit out of him. Lord Essex is to tell this to the Queen.

One follows the downfall of Essex with pitiful interest. He was not a hero only to the nation whose name he made as terrible as did Cromwell afterwards: for we are told in the "Lives of the Earls of Essex," i. 373, that his arms cut in stone were let into the walls of Cadiz, near the Puerta de Tierra. It was the spot where he had been the first to scale them; the arms were to be seen there fifty years ago, and may be there now.

Mr. Lee in the "Dictionary of National Biography" confirms this. "The intelligent, but impulsive and passionate young nobleman found in the cool and wary adviser, those qualities so different from his own which were likely to rivet his affection." Essex was indeed warmly attached to the Bacons; treachery, betrayal, blackmail, were all forgotten when the master mind made some flimsy apology, and the old confidence was at once restored as before.

In 1592 Bacon's brother Anthony was introduced by him to Essex, as having during ten years' residence abroad gained great information about foreign affairs for the use of Burleigh. He still kept touch with the able ring of intelligencers whom he had supervised in the capitals abroad, and was willing to transfer his services to Essex, with the view of ousting Burleigh from the Queen's favour, by earlier and better information. He became Essex's private secretary, at a salary of £1,000 a year, largely increased from irregular sources, and, as the number grew to five, a large staff of clerks was required. These were located at a house of Essex's at Twickenham Park, where also the Bacons resided, and which he afterwards presented to Francis. The course of business at the Scrivenery was this (Spedding, i. 250) : Anthony received all the letters, deciphered and had them fair-copied, then forwarded them, usually through Bacon, to Essex, who returned instructions from which Anthony framed, enciphered and despatched the replies. The Scrivenery was in full work on Nov. 15th, 1593, as on that day Essex sent one Lawson to Twickenham with letters to be deciphered and returned. Essex was never intrusted with the cipher—of which there are specimens on the Bacon MSS. at Lambeth Palace Library.

But at this period another person came on the scene, who plays an important part in the development of our story, in fact, without whom it would not have been written. Most of us are happily surrounded with hidden checks and restraints which, unseen, control our actions. Bacon seems to have been exempt from all but two of these; one, a kind of false shame, when, as he always was, in danger of his impecuniosity being publicly exposed; the second, the fear of his mother. This lady was one of those persons who are at one and the same time thoroughly good and equally thoroughly unpleasant. She thought nothing in 1588 of going into her son's chambers at Gray's Inn, and walking him off to Mr. Travers "lecture" (otherwise preachment) in the Temple; she ruled him with a rod of iron, and under the plea of supplying eatables for their table obtained a pretty close report of how her sons were going on from Peter, the man whom she sent up twice a week in charge thereof. She tells him that she hears he *rises* at three of the clock, not casting it out as the time he *went to bed*—somewhat like the Oxford man who, being pulled up for not attending morning chapel, told the President, " The fact is, sir, if I'm not in bed by seven o'clock, I am upset for the whole of the day."

On April 18th, 1593, she hints to Anthony the cause of Francis Bacon's great troubles, " Oh that by not hearkening to wholesome and careful good counsels and by continuing still the means of his own great hindrance he had not procured his own discredit, but had joined with God," &c.

What does this revelation as to a hindrance of long continuance, personal to Francis and in which Anthony did not share, mean? It could not be drunkenness, for in her letter of August 20th, 1594, she writes to Francis, and includes Anthony as liable to that. It could only have been " gambling," a vice, which with yet one even worse, Francis had brought with him from Paris—We shall find her anxiety reasserted in the important letter to Anthony of December 5th, 1594, "I trust they will not mime nor sinfully revel at Gray's Inn"— expressions sufficiently explained by Northbroke's evidence already quoted.

The mother had yet one more claim upon her sons. Her *whole substance had been spent upon this precious pair*. Little wonder Spenser writes to Francis in July, 1597, "no body can please her long—'and her sons be vainglorious.'" She blows off the steam in a letter to Francis of August 20th, 1590. "Let this letter be unseen: look very well to your health. Sup not nor sit up late. Surely I think your drinking to bedwards hindreth yours and your brother's digestion very much. I never knew any but sickly that used it. Observe while yet in time."

Here is a distinct charge of late drinking, against both brothers. Francis is charged with gambling as well. The influence of such a mother, commanding, and receiving such affection as to make Francis order his body to rest in her grave, with her ceaseless prying into the Gray's Inn *ménage* by the weekly visits of Peter, the cook, and his boy, was of the most powerful nature upon the brothers, and any sudden action by her would be a difficult matter to contend with openly; the only plan would be to get round it somehow.

Thus the mother's horror of stage plays amounted to a positive passion: even their neighbourhood was poisonous, and when Anthony took a house in Bishopsgate next door to a theatre, there was no peace for anyone till he removed from it.

Having now brought all our characters into the position they occupied in the autumn of 1594, both the Bacons impecunious, running a public scrivenery in touch with the stage and its actors, for which Essex paid, and horribly afraid of their termagant mother who sat upon them like a conscience.—I should like to hazard a conjecture as to Shakespeare's then position in the world. We know that he had to leave his deserted wife and children to shift for themselves, that he was so utterly moneyless as to begin by holding horses at the stage door to support himself during his informal apprenticeship as an actor, which craft does *not*, like gig-driving and farming, come by nature. How did Shakespeare live, and get on so well, as in five years to be Jack Factotum, a position needing at all events good clothes, which cost money in those days? All his biographers give it up, Halliwell only noting the sudden access of affluence in 1602 (which the writer holds to have been money paid him by Bacon when he received £1,200 for Catesby's fine). There is but one road which, with luck, in those days got a man off the ground, and sometimes made a man to sit with princes, even with the princes of the people.

It exists now! a man gets up in life through the turf, which raised the late Mr. Swindell from the position of a factory operative to the ownership of tens of thousands. From a memoir which appeared at the time of Swindell's death in the "Daily Telegraph," it appears that he started to attend a race where he had taken a 100 to 1 in crowns against a horse. But on the way to the course he had looked into a cockpit, and backed a bird of Lord Derby's (grandfather to the present peer, for it was only sixty years since) which got soundly beaten, leaving Mr. Swindell absolutely penniless. In very despair he went up to the course. The horse won, and the young mechanic continued on the turf which had saved him. It is recorded of him that he once took a house in Berkeley Square that he might sit there on Sundays and watch the callers on Mr. George Payne, or some other turf luminary, and thus guess at probable starters. There must have been great luck (natural as well as artificial) in such a character—the talents necessary for success must have been strongly present, but (I quote from memory) his biographer records some such sorrowful saying from the dying man as "Doan't 'ee let 'em saa noa worse of me than yo' can help."

"Play" is very accommodating; in Elizabeth's days there were copper "hells," as well as silver "hells," and also "hells" where £100 could be risked on a cast of the dice.

With all his wit and poetical talents, imagination and so forth, Shakespeare was a first rate man of business—he knew how to earn money, how to save it, and how to keep it; and looked sharply after his debtors and their sureties. Will anyone suggest an easier, likelier, or indeed any other means by which Shakespeare could keep himself, and his family at Stratford? put money in his purse, and obtain the costly clothing which as Jack Factotum was indispensable? Did not Crockford start as a fishmonger, and are not his bills for " Sowles " still in collectors' hands? Was he not good enough for the Duke of Wellington to be proposed and elected to the Membership of Crockys? Has not there been in our days a Prince of Monte Carlo? Was his career considered disgraceful? Disgraceful indeed! to keep a " hell!" if it be only big enough, it is not that now; and, in the days that are gone, was there not basset in the Whitehall Gallery on that Sunday evening when the worst of the Stuarts was summoned before his Judge?

Moreover women have kept banks in their own houses, not only king's mistresses, but ladies of unimpeachable rank and even character, when, as Macaulay says, all the beauties gathered round Georgiana, Duchess of Devonshire ("bless your eyes, ma'am, let me light my pipe at them," was the coster's compliment to her).

Yet she kept a gambling table—so did other

great ladies till nearly our own day, and on the fall of the last Empire did it not appear from the Police Archives that great Court ladies were recorded there as having done the same?

Sir George Trevelyan's pleasant pages have already been referred to as to the play at Brooke's Club, but they do not, I think, contain the story of the young naval officer who lost £100,000 to a professional gambler. The loser said his estate was worth as much again—and proposed to cut for double or quits. The winner said he must keep something, so suggested £90,000 instead. Amidst breathless silence the sailor won but—like Sir John Harrington, shortly to come on our scene—he never played high again, but stuck to his profession, and was one of Nelson's captains at Trafalgar.

There is *prima facie* no other way than this gambling to account for Shakespeare's rise from worse than nothing; from being a young butcher wanted for deer-stealing, to burgess, landholder, and country gentleman with coat armour. Will anyone at this point offer a better solution?

The thing was done, but how? in whatever way it came about, it was not considered a disgrace, or Greene would not have failed to cast it up to "Jack Factotum Shakespeare of the borrowed plumes."

But there happens to be positive evidence upon the point, strangely suggestive, and quite as good as, if not better than, every other accepted reference to Shakespeare. We have already quoted from Sir John Harrington, Elizabeth's godson and favourite, whom the present Bishop of London (Dictionary of National Biography — under his name) describes as "a wit and man of the world whose frankness was entire. He gives a living picture of life and society in his times, and abounds in incidental stories, which throw great light on many prominent persons." Dr. Creighton thinks, therefore, well of Sir John's keenness and accuracy.

Harrington was well versed also in games of both chance and skill and his 4th Book of Epigrams, printed in 1618, gives a list of those in vogue at the time he wrote the essay on Gambling now in question—"Seaven-up" is not named, however, among them.

What, therefore, does Harrington mean in his book "Nugæ Antiquæ" vol. i., p. 219 (edition 1804)? He is discoursing upon the wisdom of playing low stakes, which he himself acted upon from sad experience of the other thing. (I have not modernized the spelling as something turns upon it.)

"There is a great show of popularytee in playing small game—as we have heard of one that shall be nameless (because he was not blameless) that with shootynge seaven up groates among yeomen, and goinge in playne apparell, had stolen so many hartes (for I do not say he came trewly by them) that hee was accused of more than fellony." (P. 225.) "Pyrates by sea, robbers by land, have become honest substanceall men, as we call them, and purchasers of more lawfull purchas." (P. 226.) "With the ruyn of infant young gentlemen the dyeing box maintains a hungry famylee."

The deer-stealing was a very serious matter, in fact "fellony" in Elizabethan times—the food of the poor was "horsecorne" and strong laws were passed to protect fresh meat which was left unguarded. So late as 1614, Bacon, when Attorney-General, prosecuted a man in the Star Chamber for it—and could, if he so pleased, have at any time officially prosecuted Shakespeare also. No amount of friendly intimacy would have stood in the way—any more than it did with Essex—there must have been stronger reasons for a sufferance which was a practical protection. Yet Shakespeare lay very low in all his London life!—Could this be why?

Shakespeare dare not return to Stratford with this hanging over him, and though his visit to bury his son in 1596 would be overlooked, yet his return a year later to take possession of New Place would occasion much comment, especially with neighbouring gentry such as those at Combe Abbey, where there is even now a large park. The Harringtons clave to their deer as the Bagots to their ancient strain of goats, whose continuance is said to be a condition of the existence of the family itself.

The story is serious enough in all conscience, and is followed by another of the kind, of Sir John's godfather, Lord Pembroke, losing £2,000 at a sitting, because he would not reduce his stakes.

Its meaning, I submit, is this. A person of questionable repute, who had been in serious trouble for deer-stealing, was in the habit of putting on common clothes, going among yokels, and rooking them for groates at "seaven up," some kind of Vingt-et-un probably; he had by this means acquired enough money to buy real estate. His name was too risky to be safely printed. By the help of the dicing box, which he worked independently of the "seaven up," he had ruined gentlemen under age and "maintained a hungry family." He kept a copper "hell," where groats were staked, and also a silver "hell," where gentlemen could go.

1. Now several considerations flow from this. The treatise is dated 1597, the time when Shakespeare bought New Place for £60.

2. Sir John Harrington's cousin and intimate friend (afterwards Lord) Harrington was then permanently residing at Combe Abbey, his wife's inheritance, five miles from Coventry.

3. Can the purchase of the ruined home of the Cloptons at Stratford by a Stratford man "with something against him" have woke up the jealousy of feudal Combe Abbey, at which the brilliant London courtier-cousin often stayed, and called out this "shot" at Shakespeare?

4. The prudent withholding the name is suggestive, if we remember that when Greene lampooned Shakespeare in 1592, the dramatist fired up and forced Chettle to apologize for his share in the publication within a very few weeks. Evidently Harrington bore this in mind.

5. Mr. Fleay remarks that Shakespeare never appears to have visited his wife and family till his son's burial in 1596; his visit in 1597 to take "seisin" of New Place would therefore cause a stir among the gentry.

6. As bearing on the question, it is clear that Shakespeare had no more money to lay out in land till 1602, when (as I submit) he got it from the instalments of Catesby's fine paid to Bacon.

Universal as gambling was among all classes, it is odd how few are the references to it in the Plays— Shakespeare seems to shrink from it. Although public ordinaries reeked with it, and taverns as well, there are no gambling scenes!

Falstaff is not drawn as a gambler, nor are Bardolph, Pistol, etc. It could hardly fail to have been one of Prince Harry's "vanities," yet we hear nothing of it! Lastly, the terrible scenes in Pericles, with its Southwark stew which Harrington describes as the worst gambling place of all, do not echo the rattle of the dice—nothing was more common than the "cozener" at cards, yet none are produced on Shakespeare's stage. Even the line in "Love's Labour's Lost,"

"Since you can cog, I'll play no more with you."

is banter in the mouth of a lady, while Hamlet denounces it in set terms: "Gaming . . . has no relish of salvation in it."

Shakespeare evidently did not care to draw

attention to the subject, for Mr. Bartlett's admirable Concordance only records the poet's uses of gambling terms as follows;

Cog	7
Cozen	25
(Playing) Cards	5
Dice	12
Gaming	3 — All in Hamlet.
Tray trap	1 ⎫ Costermongers' Games.
Mumchance	0 ⎭
Post	0
Gleek	4
Primero	2

The whole thing is in a nut-shell. Shakespeare was a splendid man of business, worthy of the county from which he came. In addition to all his other gifts, not the least of which was sound common sense, he wanted to get on, and did so, without being very nice as to the way it was done in. He moreover kept the double life in which he lived, as dark as he could, and it was reserved for Mr. Fleay to definitely establish the existence of "the other lady," who comes out in the Sonnets.

CHAPTER III.

WE can now come to the autumn of 1594, at which time Gray's Inn, having performed no revels for three or four years, was seized with a noble desire for their renewal. It was to be a splendid affair, and got wind over all the town, which could enjoy the sumptuous outdoor procession, though it could not penetrate into the hall of performance. The Queen heard of it through Bacon first no doubt, as he had in 1589 the position of offering such a display to Lord Burleigh. He had even endeavoured to get up a masque by all the four Inns of Court, but the scheme had fallen through. Hence doubtless the discouragement which had lasted so long. It first came upon the shows; the Privy Council ordering that all plays must be licensed, so as to eliminate anything depravatory to Church and State; and the St. Paul's boys were suppressed, as interfering with bear-baiting, which the Queen desired to encourage. (Fleay, 94.) The City of London banished all theatres from its limits, and neither players nor play are heard of again in the city till 1597. In 1592 all the theatres were closed for the last half of the year on account of the Plague, and not re-opened till Christmas, 1593. The players, meanwhile, went on tour in May. No wonder, then, that in December, 1594, people gladly welcomed their return.

Now in Gray's Inn the play, according to rule, must be a classical one, translated by one of its members, and in 1564, Gascoyne had presented Euripides' "Jocasta." This, of course, was a precedent to be strictly followed in the new revival, and the play selected was Plautus' "Menæchmi," a play which Rowe, Shakespeare's first biographer, states had never before been translated into English ; going further out of his way to express his doubt whether Shakespeare knew enough Latin to read it in the original.

The play itself, moreover, would require the hand of a scholar to bring out the many fine points and perpetual contrasts of the dialogue, perfectly to the satisfaction of a houseful of Latin scholars, both of the Temple and Gray's Inn ; and it had to pass the previous censorship of an official "Master of the Revels." Indeed, Mr. Fleay, while loyally claiming the play for Shakespeare, admits the intervention of another hand. The work of that hand (if any other than his own) would be supervised by that eminent Latinist, Francis Bacon, Master of the Revels at Gray's Inn.

But in addition to the play, there was a masque, and here Mr. Spedding claims at least six of the speeches as Bacon's, and, indeed, produces the drafts in his handwriting. One of the songs was claimed by Campion, and published in his works a few years later.

There is much that calls up "Midsummer Night's Dream" about this masque, as Mr. Fleay points out (Life of Shakespeare, p. 178). Here is the last songe.

> "The houres of sleepy night decay apace,
> And now warme beds are fitter than this place;
> All time is longe that is unwilling spent,
> But hours are minutes when they yield content.
>   It is a life is never ill
>   To lye and sleepe in roses still.
>
> The rarer pleasure is, it is more sweete,
> And friends are kindest when they seldome meete;
> Who would not heare the nightingale still singe?
> Or who grew ever weary of the springe?
> The daye must have her nighte, the springe her fall,
> All is divided, none is lorde of all.
>   It were a most delightful thinge
>   To live in a perpetuall springe."

And the "dancing songe" begins:

> "Musicke is the soule of measure, speeding both in equal grace."

with a merry burden:

> "Sprightly, sprightly move your paces
> Nimbly, changing measure graces
> Lively mounted, high aspire
> For joy is only found in fyer."

Campion claimed neither of these songes in 1602. If they had been his, why did he not print them, like the former one? Can they be by the author of the six speeches? Stowe ranks him as eighth in the list of twenty-eight poets—Campion being sixth, (Camden) Shakespeare eighth—poet was playwright then. Moreover, the dialogue has a philosophical twist. The question of fishes hearing is debated, and there is much talk about magnetism, evidently based upon Dr. Gilbert's treatise, "De Magnete," published just previously, a work, we may notice, published in *Latin*, like the Plautus, from which the "Comedy of Errors" had been translated.

Now with respect to this masque, Gray's Inn had decided to turn itself into the semblance of a Court and Kingdom, and to entertain its members for twelve days playing at Kings and Councillors; with a Prince to match, for which purpose Gray's Inn Hall was filled up with a royal throne, and other regal furniture. Funds were raised by subscription from those present, and by appeals to those absent. Bacon wrote the speeches of the six Councillors, and supervised the whole. On this Spedding is clear.

The rehearsals must have occupied a month or six weeks, and while they were going on, Peter the Cook or his boy, bringing up the chicken's eggs, and "sallets," reported the approaching pageant to their mistress at Gorhambury. This was on December 5th, say three weeks before the first performance. Lady Ann Bacon became simply furious. Her dislike of stage plays was aggravated by Anthony's having taken a house next to the Bull Theatre in Bishopsgate Street, from which her continual worrying forced him to remove the following year. So she wrote him on December 5th, 1594, "I trust they will not mum nor mask or sinfully revel at Gray's Inn :" The last being the very thing the Society had decided upon doing to their heart's content, with the dice-box and wine-flask rather more accented than usual. No doubt, the figure of Lady Ann was well known in the Inn, and her servants' account of what she was capable of doing at the shortest notice, was matter of common talk in Gray's Inn, and freely canvassed in the buttery, not to speak of the Hall, to whom the discussion of her visitations to a bencher was " nuts."

As an illustration of what this terrible lady actually was suffered to do, not only with impunity but even approval, we will abstract a story from Birch. Essex had taken up again with his old flame, Lady Rutland, and on December 1st, 1596, Lady Ann, the mother of her Ladyship's secretary, actually sent him, by the channel of her said son Anthony, a letter of remonstrance upon his adultery, modelled upon those of John Knox to Mary Queen of Scots. It is both long and strong. In place of resenting, Essex meekly answered it that same day, denying the charge, but adding " Burn, I pray you." This, however, was the last thing in Lady Ann's thoughts, and, elated with her victory, she sends the whole correspondence for Anthony to read, mark, and digest. On the 6th, he thanks her for a sight of the documents which he considers " welcome and comfortable to him." Lord Essex seems to bear no malice, sends gracious compliments to his rebuker, and turns his attentions to Mrs. Bridges, a Maid of Honour, whom he got into serious trouble with the Queen by them.

When, therefore, this terrible virago wrote on December 5th, 1594, to her son Anthony, "I trust they will not mum or mask or sinfully revel at Gray's Inn. Who were sometimes counted first, God grant they wane not daily and deserve to be named last," the contingency had to be distinctly faced, of Lady Bacon's putting in a personal appearance, with a row of the first magnitude to follow on between her and the assembled guests. It is to be noted that the epithet "counted first" is used elsewhere by Anthony as if it were a house or pet name of his brother Francis. Everything was going on merrily, Gray's Inn Hall filling up with thrones, scaffolding and seats, rich hangings covering the walls, nymphs and fairies practising pleasant melody with viols and voices, and gentlemen marching and counter-marching in the rehearsals; when down came the bolt from the blue; what time Peter the Cook, who had duly reported at Gorhambury the great doings in preparation at Gray's Inn, brought up to Anthony together with the pigeons, the following note: "December 5th,

1594. I trust they will not mum nor mask nor sinfully revel at Gray's Inn. Who were sometimes counted first, God grant they wane not daily, and deserve to be counted last." The allusion to Francis was pointed, as " one to be counted first " is used for Francis in one of Anthony's own letters.

The screw came down very heavily, and on a very tender place.

From a letter five days later from Bacon to Anthony, sending him a bond for £600 for his signature, and apologizing for its being £100 more than the brother had agreed to become surety for, it is plain that neither brother seems to have had a penny in his pockets, and it must have been a trial for Anthony to know that the original £500 had been paid for a jewel, which evidently had been parted with, and was no longer available for money raising. Where had it gone to ? Bacon had been already arrested for £300, the price of a jewel! The pinch was a terrible one, for Anthony was already bound to Fleetwood, the late Recorder of London, for £100 on Bacon's behalf. This judge was probably a relation, having resided at Bacon House, Foster Lane, but, as he had deceased on the previous February 28th, his people would probably be looking after their money, from which Bacon " promised immediately to free " his brother.

Under these circumstances to offend the only person from whom the brothers could obtain a penny, was impossible. As was also the stopping the performance. "It was too late for praying," says Mr. Spedding—though doubtless Anthony would seek to again appease his mother by stating that Psalms XXXV. and XXXVI. were "the very joy of his heart." All that could be done was to deny all authorship of the pieces, as the only possible chance of avoiding Lady Ann's personal appearance on the scene—and her fame for prompt action was as great as that of a former landlady of the "Anglers" at Marlow, who, when all the men about her recoiled from the task, had with her own hands "chucked out" of the tap a six foot drunken bargee, the terror of the river; the hostess standing four feet eleven, and scaling seven stone nine.

Among similar MacStingers were Sarah Sophia Whilome, Countess of Jersey, and the late Mrs. "Diamond" Hope, a daughter of Napoleon's General Rapp, and sole inheritress of the unrivalled paternal powers of swearing. An eminent solicitor friend of mine, the late Mr. Michael Abrahams, described her as the "only *man* he ever was afraid of."

The Temple Ambassador had arrived in great state, and been conducted to the Prince's presence with sound of trumpet. The performance was ready to begin "before a splendid company of lords, ladies, and worshipful personages, that did expect some notable performance," when the stage was stormed by the back-seat people, who had dined at one o'clock, and diverted themselves since by the dice-box and the wine cup freely passed round. The performance could not go on —so the Temple envoy with his train withdrew in high dudgeon, and, after an attempt to quiet down matters with dancing and revelling, the players were called upon to "play the audience out, with the play they had performed before the Court that afternoon,"—the historian goes on to say "the night begun and continued to the end in nothing but confusion and error," whereupon it was ever afterwards called the "Night of Errors." The play, hitherto unnamed, received this name of "Errors" from the circumstances under which it was performed and as such remained a stock piece of the Theatre Company. As for the Masque, it was at once dropped out of sight, and replaced the next week by a splendid device to celebrate the restoration of amity between the offended Templars and Gray's Inn. In this Mr. Spedding opines that Bacon had a leading hand. Why his name was kept entirely out of it has already been explained.

Nor did the brothers again risk the loss of their only friend, though on October 15th, 1596, Bacon wrote from Gray's Inn to Lord Shrewsbury "to borrow a horse and armour for some public show," as if he were a professional director of such things.

Bacon's vices and extravagance kept him miserably poor till 1608, when a wealthy marriage, the falling in of his Star Chamber Reversion, and his fees as Solicitor-General, lifted him from the slough of despond in which his life till then had been passed, so that the mother's displeasure (she lived till 1610, though probably insane) barred Bacon from all avowed connection with the stage—the scrivenery trade being, however, carried on, on "the quiet," as we shall see hereafter.

Of course Royal and Inns of Court Masques would still continue, and I was anxious to trace any possible connection of Bacon with the production of "Twelfth Night," at the cost of the Middle Temple Benchers, in their Hall in February, 1602. The Gray's Inn Master of the Revels could not fail, however, to have been at least a guest—if only as a *distraction* from the pressure of creditors who had just compelled him to mortgage Twickenham Park. I regret, however, that my Benchers have now twice refused me access to the Inn Records of the period, and, if I have thus overlooked any material fact, the blame must rest with the Treasurers of the Middle Temple for 1894 and 1896.

Still the Gray's Inn Masques and the Scrivenery hereafter described, would keep up a close intimacy, and even respect, between Bacon and Shakespeare; and our next evidence is at a time when Bacon had become Attorney-General. The story is a sickening one, and short preface is required to it.

The infamous Carre was about to be married to

the equally infamous Lady Frances Howard, the divorced wife of the son of Bacon's murdered patron Essex. Bacon had squirmed to Carre in order to obtain the Mastership of the Wards and had failed. He therefore tried before the wedding to curry favour by offering to provide a Masque similar to the gorgeous pageant produced by the Inner Temple and Gray's Inn on the occasion of the marriage of the Elector Palatine and the Princess Elizabeth on February 14th, 1613. These Masques were usual on such occasions. At the week's festivities which took place at the marriage of the Prince of Orange with Charles I.'s daughter (whose son was to dethrone the Stuarts), a great scaffolding for the show was erected outside Whitehall Banqueting House. During that whole week Strafford lay awaiting his doom, vainly imploring the King, for whose service he was about to die, and whose protection had previously been promised him, to refuse to sign the Attainder. The mills of God do not always grind slowly, for within eight years that same scaffold was re-erected on the same spot, and the King himself ascended it.

As will be seen, Bacon absolutely tried to get the Masque performed by the four Inns of Court. But three of these bodies had an instinct that both bride and bridegroom would be in the Tower as convicted murderers within a very short period, and held aloof. So Bacon by a letter in his own hand, thus commits his own Inn.

"It may please your good L. I am sorry the joint masque from the four Inns of Court faileth. Nevertheless because it falleth out that at this time Gray's Inn is well furnished of gallant young gentlemen, your L. may be pleased to know that rather than this occasion shall pass without some demonstration of affection from the Inns of Court, there are a dozen gentlemen of Gray's Inn that out of the honour which they bear to your Lordship and my Lord Chamberlain (father of the bride) *to whom at their last masque they were so much bounden*, will be ready to furnish a masque, wishing it were in their power to perform it according to their minds."

If Mr. Spedding, who publishes this (vol. iv., p. 394), had only glanced back to the Masque of Flowers in 1594, he would have discovered the Bacon-Shakespeare sodality thirty years ago!

As a matter of fact Gray's Inn found only the composers and performers, the cost (some £2,000 then, £14,000 now), being borne by Bacon personally.

The expression, the Gentlemen of Gray's Inn were "much bounden" to the Lord Chamberlain at their last masque seems to indicate some kind of sociality between that Inn and the Players. Indeed one of them, Ben Jonson, was Bacon's guest at York House on the proudest day of his life—his sixtieth birthday—an honour the poet repaid by sympathy, and saying all that could be said, by way of defence, when the terrible downfall came, and almost the only thing Bacon, who was as little as he was great, could say was that he had *not* received as much as £100,000 in bribes during his Chancellorship. If such generous acts as these were common with the bricklayer poet, we can well understand the casual visitor recording his merits on his gravestone:

"OH RARE BEN JONSON."

CHAPTER IV.

THE SCRIVENERY.

BACON'S brother Anthony, before referred to, was employed by his uncle, Lord Burleigh, to travel on the Continent, as a "political intelligencer," from 1579 to 1592, in which year he returned to England in bad health, and he applied to his uncle for a post at Court, but was for some reason disappointed. He kept, however, in full touch with his foreign correspondents, and seems also to have established a Scriptorium where he copied books for sale. Thus (Birch, i. 85) Standen writes that by one Lawson, he sends his travels in Turkey, Italy, and Spain—"nothing too high in prices for you"—out of which and the Zibaldone MS. Anthony is to copy what he likes. If Standen discovers a lost MS. (his discourse on the Spanish State), Anthony shall have it.

Morgan Colman, an English correspondent, writes on September 23rd, 1692, that he is feeding himself with his papers, which he trusts will deliver fruit well pleasing to Anthony.

At this time he was introduced by his brother Francis to the young Earl of Essex, to whom

Anthony found his brother "bound and in deep arrearges," otherwise heavily in debt: but yet possessing the enormous influence which a strong mind has over an impetuous and weaker one. He recommended Anthony as being of skilled ability in matters of state, especially foreign, and hence likely to obtain earlier foreign intelligence for Essex than the Queen's advisers were likely to receive—thus enabling the Earl to conciliate the Queen's favour by intelligence in advance of that procured by the Cecils.

A Scrivenery is, of course, a prime factor in such a service, and the engagement of correspondents upon the Continent proceeded at once. It was originally started, no doubt, in Gray's Inn, but the Scrivener's Company had a monopoly which they strictly enforced; hence it was removed to Twickenham Park, a house belonging to Lord Essex, as being out of the reach of the City Company's franchises, while the brothers Bacon occasionally resided there, and it ultimately became, by the Earl's free gift, the property of Bacon. On April 4th, 1591, Palmer, Burleigh's correspondent at St. Luz, is applied to for copies of his letters to Burleigh. In the same month a survey of Essex's parks with their value is "faired out." It is at Lambeth, and is beautifully done. In fact, if my copy of the "Apologie" (and we know from Bacon's words on Essex's trial that it was written there), be an average example of the work, the writers must have been masters of their craft, it being " without a blot " as were the " true originall copies " from which Heminge and Condell compiled the First Folio.

On September 15th, 1593, Phelips (Walsingham's decipherer of intercepted letters) is retained on the staff, and the cipher is only known to him, Standen, and the brothers Bacon, not communicated to their employer—Essex.

The number of paid agents in connection with this " news agency " was enormous, the chief being an exceedingly clever spy, named Standen, who boasted that he could come and go as a Frenchman. He began his trade in 1562 and became a Spanish pensioner. Walsingham bought him for £100 in 1572, the King of Spain paying him concurrently 480 crowns. In 1590 he was detected and lay eight months in prison, from which Anthony procured his release by bribery. Coming to England, he appealed to Burleigh for employment as a spy, which he obtained, afterwards being retained by Essex as well. Knighted by Elizabeth for some unheard-of reason, he betrayed James I.'s secrets in 1604, was thrown into the Tower, and nearly lost his life. The list of correspondents, apparently all paid in meal or in malt, is over thirty in number: comprising English Ambassadors to France, Holland, and the States General, French Protestant Ministers, agents sent specially on Essex's behalf, Guicciardini, the historian, Mr.

Bodley—hereafter as Sir Thomas to found the Bodleian Library—shipmasters, and a most extraordinary ganglion in Scotch affairs.

Essex had his own agent at Edinburgh—he corresponded with Bower, the English ambassador there, some of the rebel lords, and the Scotch Chancellor; while, on the other hand, one Foulis actually bribed Anthony himself in the interest of the Scotch king. The imbroglio is such, that it is by no means wonderful to learn that Lord Northampton goes to Essex's bedside on June 28th, 1599, and informs him that unless he there and then makes over Essex's House, where they then were, as a free gift to his secretary, Anthony Bacon, that individual will place in the hands of Secretary Cecil the whole of his intrigues with the Scotch king. Essex has no resource but to comply, and the estate, valued at £2,000, became Anthony's, though subsequently redeemed by a "whip" of from £2,000 to £4,000 among the family: an effort called up by Elizabeth's outspoken anger at the proceeding. This was matter of common talk, and Wotton's relation of this infamous treachery is corroborated by Chamberlain—which last upsets Mr. Spedding's faint attempt to discredit Wotton, himself one of Essex's secretaries.

Of course the expense of all this was enormous. From Devereux, "Lives of the Devereux," vol. i., p. 295, we learn that one of his agents writes Essex that Mr. Edmondes has been paid £300 for his journey to Lyons, and 600 crowns more since his return, and asks for instructions, as this is much more than the Queen allows her agents. How, then, were funds found for all this? Wotton, at one time one of his five secretaries, tells us that Essex received from Elizabeth more than £300,000 besides the fees of his offices, three in number—as Earl Marshal, General of the Horse and of the Ordnance, and the sums spent for war purposes. This last office was over £1,000 a year, and it was but the third in money value. It was nothing for the vain old hag of sixty to give her favourite £7,000 in cochineal. But dividing the sums quoted by Wotton over thirteen years, 1588-1600, we get, at a small estimate, £32,000, or in our present currency, £210,000 a year, of which he is said to have allowed Anthony £1,000. Bacon's own rapacity knew no bounds, and yet, like all other spendthrifts, he never had a farthing in his pocket.

We have now to give some particulars as to the mentions of the Scrivenery on this matter. We have seen that it was used for copying out MSS. from Standen and Colman, and that a MS. relating to Italy was stolen out of Lord Essex's chamber; so that other work was taken on besides Lord Essex's.[1]

Anthony writes Francis from Gorhambury on November 15th, 1593, that Lawson was just arrived from the Earl (who had sent for him ex-

[1] Spedding, vol. i., p. 349.

pressly from Twickenham), with letters from Dr. Morison (Essex's agent at Edinburgh), and a most earnest request to return them, deciphered, with all possible expedition.

The next is from Francis to Anthony, dated "Twickenham Park, this 25th of January, 1594-5. I have here an idle pen or two, specially one that was cozened, thinking to have got some money this term: I pray send me somewhat else for them to write out beside your Irish collection, which is almost done. There is a collection of Dr. James, largeliest of Flanders, which though it be no great manner, yet I would be glad to have it."

This Dr. James had been chaplain to Lord Leicester, was then Dean of Christchurch, and was a voluminous writer. He succeeded the father of Bacon's young friend, Toby Matthew, as Bishop of Durham in 1606.

Going back to the letter, it states plainly that he is short of "copy" at the scrivenery, that one of his clerks (who had been cheated, and, therefore, probably came cheap) was worrying for work— hence Anthony was to look out to see if he could get any of Dr. James's copying. Bacon, like every other tradesman, kept an eye on quarters where custom was to be had.

The next reference we find is in August, 1596. Essex had prepared "a true relation of the action at Cadiz," sent it home by his secretary Cuffe, who writes to Anthony: "The original you are to keep, because my Lord charged me to cause either you or Mr. Fontaine (minister of the French Church) to turn either the whole or the sum of it into French, and to cause it to be sent to some good personage in these parts, under a false name or anonymously. (Anthony was rather partial to these anonymous letters, and one is extant from him to the Countess of Northumberland, Essex's sister, informing her of her husband's adultery.) The Queen was very angry, and forbade Cuffe on pain of death to have it printed, whereupon Anthony, finding he could not get it put into type, resolved to write out and send abroad copies of it, so that they would very shortly pass into all parts and speak all languages in spite of those who sought to suppress them."

Anthony did his part for Scotland, Mr. Bodley, afterwards of the library, for the Low Countries, and M. Fontaine for France.

The Liège spy informs us it occupied three long written sheets.

The next allusion is to the "Apologie," which will be more conveniently taken as a whole in the next chapter.

To proceed. During the years 1591-1602, one Topcliffe was a diligent discoverer and violent persecutor of Roman Catholics under the penal laws. Elizabeth seems to have given credit to his reports, and encouraged him. In March, 1599, there seem to have been heavy complaints against him for arresting Harrison, one of Cecil's spies, and he would seem to have got into such disgrace, as to make him draw up a supplication (probably to the Queen), which was evidently of interest. It must have been written before Anthony's death, about May 27th, 1601, and it shows how keen Bacon was to earn anything, however small. It runs thus:

"Good brother, I send you the supplication which Mr. Topcliffe lent me. It is curiously written and worth the writing out for the art, though the argument be bad. But it is lent me but for two or three days. So God keep you."

If my conjecture is accurate as to the person, he was subsequently reinstated; for he assists Chief Justice Popham in some examinations in the following year. On the other hand, it is equally possible that the supplicant may have been one Charles Topcliffe, who, at the loot of Cadiz, carried off £600 in silver (£4,200 now), and pleaded that it was the private property of the Corregidor, by whose wife it was given him! But the fact remains the same. Bacon was greedy for "copy," and did not trouble himself about the author's consent before publishing it.

Oddly enough, the last instance we shall find of this is in 1608, at which time the Scrivenery was still used for theatre purposes, the last of Shakespeare's plays appearing some two years later. In 1608 Bacon composed a notebook of private memoranda of his property, and his plans for the future, which Professor Rawson Gardner describes as a thorough insight into his character. It is a very pitiable record, and it is hardly conceivable that it could have been written by the man who wrote any of the published works.

Its full title is " Comentarius Solutus sive Pandecta sive Ancilla Memoriæ." It was discovered by Mr. Spedding in 1848, in Archbishop Tenison's Library at St. Martin's-in-the-Fields and is now in the British Museum. It seems to have taken Bacon a week to write it, and it occupies some fifty-five pages of print in Spedding's vol. iv., p. 40.

He reckons his property as worth £24,000 (clear of debts), his income as £4,975 (say £35,000 of it in our money), so that he was not a needy man; but he thinks only of ingratiating himself with the King by flattering his domestics and physicians, and of noting all the weaknesses of the Attorney-General, with a view of superseding him. It is a pitiful record of grasping human selfishness, without one redeeming part.

Though his mother was living, her name never occurs, but two entries are so peculiar that even Mr. Spedding in a note gives to them the right explanation, though dissenting from it. The old Lord Treasurer Dorset had died suddenly two months before, leaving a widow over seventy, and some eight children. The first memorandum is (Spedding, iv. 3) " to send messages of compliment to my Lady Dorsett' 'the wydow.'" The second, "Applying myself to be inward with my Lady Dorsett per Champnes ad utilitat testam" (Spedding, iv. 35). Spedding agrees that these last words stand for use of the will, and, after much speculation as to how Bacon was to get his profit, adds in a note a friend's suggestion that they relate to some professional employment in connection with that document. It really was in order to obtain the scrivener work in connection with what we should call the executorship. This work was highly paid, and the London scriveners throve exceedingly, so the Solicitor-General chose to tout for the work by an agent, no doubt his servant.

We have now linked together all the facts at present traceable with regard to this writing shop. That copying was costly and very profitable work the sudden leap of printing into common use a century before distinctly proves; that these Scrivenery conductors would take up any work, however obtained, whether in confidence or not, is also perfectly clear, as is, unhappily, the fact that they were crippled with debts, and borrowed from everyone they could. Would Bacon, for a quarter of a century Master of the Revels at Gray's Inn, not ask Shakespeare for loans, when on his good will depended the retention of the Inn pageant work, for which the other theatre companies were eager?

Chamberlain tells us that Sir Francis Bacon was the chief "contriver" of the Masque on the marriage of the Palatine, which came by water from Winchester Place, close by the Globe Theatre, where the Templars and Gray's Inn men who produced it had been drilled and formed up. The water pageant alone cost £300. The pickings in copying out the parts of such a pageant would be worth having.

Dare Shakespeare refuse the loans and risk the loss of the connection?

Emphatically no; but the Scrivenery could copy out his prompters' parts and actors' copies from the MS. plays taken down from his dictation, keep them in order for use, and, when required, the cost would go "to my account with you," *i.e.*, Bacon.

Shakespeare, from his two avocations (for the utter silence of the plays on the question of gambling is strong evidence that he carried them on concurrently), had more money to lend than he could find borrowers for, hence employed agents to make loans for him. He knew how to keep as well as to make money—actors did this in those days, witness Burbage, Alleyne, and Henslow. But he also looked sharp after his debtors, and in the meagre annals of his life but one fact repeats itself three times, and that is: his suing his debtors and their surety, one of them, too, a fellow townsman.

Here, then, we have the place where the priceless manuscripts of the plays would be kept under the control of Lord Bacon, at all events up to 1608. What became of them afterwards may possibly be told hereafter.

CHAPTER V.

THE APOLOGIE.

IN the spring of 1598 the French king concluded a separate peace with Spain, and opinions were greatly divided in England as to the advisability of Elizabeth doing the same. Supported by Burleigh, it was bitterly opposed by Essex, who accordingly prepared a document, addressed: " An Apologie for the Erle of Essex against those who Falsely and Maliciously say him to be the onelie Hindrance of the Peace of his Country."

At the end of my copy of this " Apologie," which is dated April 8, 1600, there are " Considerations against the Peace" (with Spain), etc., with some prayers, which I believe, for reasons set out in " The Academy " of April 13th, 1895 (*vide* Appendix), to have been written at the Scrivenery for the private use of the unhappy Essex at his request. The book seems always to have been under Bacon's control, as he admits in his " Apologie" for his conduct to Essex.

The Queen disliked this appeal to the public, and treated him coolly in consequence. When next at Court, in the heat of dispute, the Earl, with a gesture of contempt, turned his back upon Elizabeth, saying "her conditions were as crooked as her carcase," whereupon the Queen boxed his ears, and told him to go "in malam rem." And a "bad thing" he went in for there and then, putting his hand to his sword, swearing that he would not bear such an indignity from Henry VIII., and leaving the Court. A great coolness ensued; a letter of Lord Essex to Lord Keeper Egerton added fuel to the fire, and Bacon brought this last up against Essex on the proceedings in June, 1600, as bold, presumptuous, and derogatory to Her Majesty—going on to say that it had been published by the Earl's friends, of whom the brothers Bacon, by the way, were at that time the chief, and ran the Scrivenery where the copies had been translated and written out.

Camden and other historians distinctly say that, although the quarrel was apparently patched up in the following October, from this time dated Essex's fall.

For the Bacons translated this "Apologie" into French, had it copied at the Scrivenery, and distributed in Italy, France, and Spain, causing there great irritation by its outspoken language about the King. Spaniards marvelled that such libels, sent by the Earl to Mr. Bacon, should be allowed by Elizabeth to be written in her country, "*making comedies and jests of the King of Spain upon stages.*" These are the words written from Liège by Petit, a spy, under date June 10th, 1599, extant in the

"Domestic State Papers," vol. 270, and it is extraordinary that he should credit Anthony with the same power of making people ridiculous upon the stage, which Essex later on attributes to him. It must have been a matter of common notoriety to be circulating at the same time in both London and Liège. The spy says that a copy had been sent to the King of Spain, as if Standen had turned it into Spanish.

Things looked gloomy at this time for Essex and his parasites the Bacons. He had forfeited the Queen's favour, and made things worse by his goings on with the Maids of Honour, with four of whom he was credited with intimacy at the same time. Two of them, named Bridges and Russell, were driven from Court by the Queen with oaths and blows.

Essex was committed to custody in September, 1599, and for eight months confined to his house. He was in debt, and though the fees of his great offices regularly came in, yet none of such princely gifts as the £7,000 in cochineal were now to be looked for from the Queen. On the contrary, his monopoly of sweet wines, which had expired at Michaelmas, was not renewed, but fell into the Exchequer. The Bacons, too, were at their wits' end. In March, 1600, Francis Bacon had begged Elizabeth for a gift in fee simple of three parcels of Crown Land, value £80 odd, on the grounds that his brother was being forced to sell Gorhambury; and on another plea, in order to free himself from "the contempt of the contemptible that measure a man by his estate"—his creditors were evidently getting rude to him. The request was certainly not granted by Elizabeth.

In January, 1600, suits were pending against Bacon, and on January 25th he applies to his old creditor Hickes for a further loan of £200, on sureties whose consent he says he had not asked. Anthony, by a threat to divulge Essex's intrigues with the King of Scots (who was next heir to the throne) to Cecil, obtained a gift of Essex House (all, apparently, Essex had left at his disposal), which had to be ransomed afterwards for £4,000.

This terrible treachery by a pampered and trusted servant is attested by both Wotton and Chamberlain, the last in "Domestic State Papers," 1599, p. 222. Anthony, probably from shame and remorse, appears to have destroyed all his correspondence with Essex, for the valuable series in Lambeth Palace Library, from which so much of this monograph has been derived, and from which much more is evidently derivable, ceases here.

Crippled with debts, insulted by creditors who are pressing him, all other resources gone, with the Queen obdurate, and the Cecils hostile, it seems to have struck Bacon that, if nothing was to be gained by *Essex's life*, his *death* and *forfeiture* would be of value to those who brought it about, to whom such things were afterwards commonly granted by the Crown; and, in the spring of 1600, the scheme was put in hand. Essex's sister, Lady Rich, had at the end of July addressed a letter to the Queen, interceding for her brother. It may be seen in Birch, ii. 442, and is certainly slightly blasphemous as well as "piquant," the term used for it by Bacon on the Earl's trial. It seems, however, to have intensely irritated Elizabeth, and accordingly the Bacons issued several copies from the Scrivenery, which ended in Lady Rich's being summoned twice before the Council to answer for it—the usual prelude to committal to the Tower. And to make matters worse, the half-forgotten "Apologie" which had caused the original quarrel ending on the box upon the ears, was maliciously prefixed to it!

It had probably been asked for by Essex himself, whom illness had made very despondent (Chamberlain speaks of him on February 28th, 1600, as "somewhat crazie" and March 5th as "quite out of minde") and religiously inclined; as the beautiful copy without a blot made for him at the Scrivenery, and now in my possession, dated April 8th and 10th 1600, contains some prayers as for a sick man. But early in May it got secretly printed with Lady Rich's letter appended, and the result came quite up to the expectation of the conspirators; Elizabeth became furious, put two men into close prison, and had the copies sought for, but only 8 out of 200 issued could be found. Two important extracts are inserted here verbatim from the Sydney Papers.[1]

Whyte to Sir Robert Sydney on May 10th, 1600.

"An apology written by my Lord of Essex about the Peace is I hear printed on which his Lordship is very much troubled, and hath sent to my Lord of Canterbury, and others and to the Stationers to suppress them, for it is done without his knowledge or procurement, and he fears it may be ill taken, two are committed close prisoners; what they will disclose is not yet known.

"The Queen is offended that this Apology of Peace is printed for of 200 Copies only 8 is heard of—it is said that my Lady Rich's letter to Her Majesty is also printed which is an exceeding wrong donne to the Earle of Essex."

Essex was in despair, seeing the malignity of the move, and at once wrote to the Archbishop—as Press licencer, and the Stationers' Company to stop the sale—a process accomplished by May 28th, as Chamberlain tells us.

Essex had, however, on the 20th, written to the Queen in terms which tells us a secret hitherto known only to the spy at Liége, as we have seen.

"I am subject to their wicked information that first envied me for my happiness in your favour,

[1] "Calendar Domestic State Papers," p. 149, May 13th, 1600.

and now hate me out of custom, but as if I were thrown into a corner like a dead carcase I am gnawed on and torn by the vilest and basest creatures upon earth. . . . *Already they print me*, and make me speak to the world, and shortly they will play me *in what form they list upon the stage.* The least of these is a thousand times worse than death."

Now Bacon had thrown him aside like a dead dog—had laid, and was prosecuting the information against the Earl for his Irish conduct. On this point public opinion was strongly clear. *Bacon had certainly printed the " Apologie " and Lady Rich's letter.*

Do the lines emphasized mean that *Bacon* had control of a theatre, and could cause a play to be written and acted upon the stage to Essex's prejudice? The inference when coupled with that from the Liége letter, seems hard to avoid. It must be remembered that the Earl was a popular favourite, and that for long afterwards all pamphlets in his defence were suppressed by Government.

If this doubly vouched statement be correct, we have Bacon in command of the Globe Theatre, and in such authority there as to be able to risk its popularity with playgoers to serve his own private ends.

But the hideous story must go on, for it is hard to believe Shakespeare does not come in again.

Essex died a death worthy of the man whose arms even yet remain on the walls of Cadiz to mark the spot where he was the first to scale them. Anthony died of remorse within four months, so deep in debt and disgrace that it is due only to these circumstances that Chamberlain records his decease, as being of no benefit to his hard-pressed brother Francis.

In the autumn come the fines and ransoms of the prisoners, and from Catesby's fine of 4,000 marks, £1,200, payable by instalments, was assigned to Bacon by the Queen's order. He forthwith writes to his creditor Hickes, who had probably just jogged his memory ; grumbling at the smallness of the amount, and promising to attend to him sometime this vacation, "which then ran on till November 2nd," four months' respite.

Catesby's instalments could hardly be spread over less than six months, and in the spring of the next year comes that sudden flush of money to Shakespeare, which Mr. Halliwell (Outlines, vol. i., p. 240) is astonished at, and which Mr. Fleay passes unnoticed. Now the previous windfall in Shakespeare's life was the £60 paid in 1597 for New Place, and which Sir John Harrington accounts for as " landed " from the ruin of an infant young gentleman. That haul he at once put away in lands, and at this time the dramatist purchased the Combe Lands for £320, buys up a blot on the title of New Place (which may up to then have kept him out of possession), and a copy-hold at Rowington. This last speaks of the determination to invest the whole of the money, common in minds to whom a big pull is a luxury to be thoroughly enjoyed, and put away safely. It is the act of a man occupying a risky position, who, like Louis Phillipe or Napoleon III., invested as much as he could get in the English Funds with the remark, "That's safe at all events." Not that the Empress Eugénie's jewels, sold piecemeal to the native princes of India, did not realize half a million more.

Many other gamblers, whether in politics, stock exchange, even racing and betting, have done the like, and a thousand times as many have wished, when too late, they had done the same while they had the chance.

My submission is that this money, say at least £600, was worried out of Bacon by Shakespeare, who knew his debtor's only fetchable point, "the contempt of the contemptible," and traded upon that at the right moment, promptly putting the money away in a safe quarter where the shifty debtor could not get it back, however much he might try it on.

One more association between the two men is adducible. Did Bacon write the epitaph upon Shakespeare prefixed to the Second Folio of 1632?

In Bacon's "Life of Henry VII." published in 1622, pages 247 and 248, there appears as the concluding sentence an epitaph upon that king;

and in the Second **Folio** of Shakespeare, published in 1632, appears the "epitaph on the Admirable Dramatick Poet, Mr. William Shakespeare."

Both passages have, as their author's last thought, and as their closing line, the reflection that a man is more richly sepulchred in a written monument of his fame, than in any material tomb, however sumptuous or even regal it may be. The idea is Horace's :

"Exegi monumentum aere perennius,"

and therefore familiar to a scholar with a fine ear for rhythm and swing. Such learning was common enough among the courtiers of "King Elizabeth," and the example of George Buchanan had kept it alive in the reign of Scotch "Jamie."

Let us see how it is worked out in these two books, published within ten years of each other.

"The Epitaph on the Admirable Dramatick Poet Mr. William Shakespeare" (2nd. 3rd. and 4th Folios).	Bacon, "Henry VII." pp. 247-248, conclusion.
"What needs my Shakespeare for his Hallowed Bones? A pyramid of earth in piled stones. Or that his mortal relics should be hid Beneath some starre-y-pointing pyramid? Dear Son of Memory, great Heir of Fame, Why needs the world such witness of thy Name?	"*He lyeth buried at* Westminster *in one of* the Statelyest and Daintiest Monuments *of* Europe *both for the* Chappell, *and for the* Sepulcher. *So that hee dwelleth more richly* Dead *in the* Monument *of his* Tombe, *than he did* Alive *in* Richmond *or any of his*

Thou in our wonder and astonishment
Hast built thyself a lasting monument,
And so sepulchred in such state dost lie,
That Kings for such a tomb would wish to die."

Palaces. *I could wish he did the like, in this* Monument *of his* Fame."

Now this epitaph dates itself to a nicety ; it is a burst of warm, heart-felt affection for a friend, thrown off just after Shakespeare's burial, and before the precise shape of the present monument at Stratford, the only one of his own time which exists, had been decided on ; nay, at the time while it was being debated among friends and admirers of his genius as to the erecting a monument.

Let us spot two phrases in the epitaph—" my Shakespeare," and " our wonder and astonishment." They are perfectly natural ones; but as to this epitaph for a man whose social talents made so firm a mark in the memory of his epitaphist, that he could keep it by him for the next sixteen years, why came these lines, full as they are of almost Miltonian music, to be left out of the first edition of 1623 and yet appear in the second edition of 1632 ? Surely there must have been some cause for the omission of this tribute of an affectionate friend of such commanding genius from the First Folio, which had ceased to exist when the Second saw the light! Ben Jonson's rugged tribute could be prefixed, but why should this still grander one be left out? During that nine years between 1623 and 1632, the restraint, whatever it was, vanished. Why?

To go on with our microscoping of the epitaph—let us look closely into its composition—the writer must have been a man in years, and of grave and sober habits of thought to have imagined and given utterance to such grand organ music—resembling Milton's "Lycidas" and Tennyson's "In Memoriam," where also, after long lapse of years, the loss of a personal friend, one's other self, is bewailed. Moreover the writer had first learnt to use his pen in pre-Jacobean days, from his using the word "starre-y-pointing," the "y" prefix being in common use about the middle of the sixteenth century and dying out before its close.

The upshot, therefore, seems, so far, to be this: that the writer of the epitaph was a scholar with the classics at his fingers' ends; courtier: a man of taste; personal friend and appreciator of Shakespeare's wit; and brought up in traditions of the middle of Elizabeth's reign at latest. All of which would imply familiar knowledge of that poet of whom it is written:

> "Horace still charms with graceful negligence,
> And, without method, wins us into sense;
> Can, like a friend familiarly convey
> The truest doctrines in the easiest way,
> Yet judged with coolness though he sang with fire;"

and this knowledge could hardly have been acquired by a youth who, having learnt at a grammar school small Latin and less Greek, was bound apprentice to a butcher when thirteen years old.

De Missy in his "Notes on Anacreon" quotes a passage from Shakespeare to show that the Author of the Plays had a knowledge of Greek.

It is in " Timon," Act IV., Scene 7.

"The sun's a thief and with his great attraction
Robs the vast sea. The moon's an arrant robber,
And her pale fire she snatches from the sun.
The sun's a thief whose liquid surge resolves
The moon into salt tears."

(Pseud.) "Anacreon," Ode XIX., runs thus:

πίνει θάλασσα δ' αὔρας
Ὁ δ' ἥλιος θάλασσην
τὸν δ' ἥλιον σελήνη,

which I roughly condense, sacrificing everything to literalness and metre

"Deeply drinks the dark brown field,
Drinks of it the tree-clad weald.
Drinks the sun from ocean streams,
Drinks of him the pale moon-beams,
Drinks the sea from showers of sky,
All things drink, mates, why not I?"

A perfect drinking song with a rollick about it that would find acceptance with roystering classical topers in those classical days which lasted certainly down to Porson's

οὔτε τόδε οὔτε τἄλλο.

In these unclassical days may I explain this last

jest? The drunken pillar of Greek scholarship at Cambridge had seen both liquor and candles simultaneously give out, and his comment reads in his mother tongue,

"Out e tallow out e toddy."

My letter to "The Academy" of March 23rd, 1895 evoked no contradiction, but I learn from an amiable friend at the head of Gray's Inn Library, that since my establishment of the sodality of Bacon and Shakespeare, a tradition is creeping up that the summer house in the Gray's Inn Gardens, beneath the famous elms which this so great (and oh, so little) man planted, was the scene of some of these drinking symposia between the two. My copy of the "Apologie," which must have touched his hand when he presented it to his victim Essex, rested some days next to the fine portrait there of the man to whom Humanity owes a debt which can never be discharged.

This epitaph business chimes in too well with what we unhappily know of the character of Bacon.

In the taverns where the actors assembled, much sorrow would be felt when the death of Shakespeare was announced, and the feeling, then as now, would be to raise a monument over him as over any comrade of note who had joined the majority. As often as not these schemes collapsed, as was the case with Ben Jonson's, where subscriptions freely promised at the outset, failed lamentably before the work was ordered, or rather, not ordered at all. One cannot doubt that a subscription for Shakespeare's memorial would be at once set on foot, and that application would first be made to the Lord Chancellor Bacon, probably by his friend Ben Jonson, to head the list with something handsome. Imagine the disgust of the assembled troupe, when the reply came back, that the deceased needed no monument except his splendid works, and inclosing only a copy of verse expressing this idea. Such a substitute for a subscription would thoroughly damp the project from the very first, and the whole thing would fall through, to be revived some dozen years later, when a Dutch sculptor living in Southwark could be employed to cut the now existing memorial over the grave.

The epitaph was held over at the time of the publication of the First Folio in 1623. Bacon's name was then an object of popular detestation, and even when inserted in the volume of 1632, his name was suppressed as being no recommendation.

I have now for some two years been patiently unveiling, from his mother's and his brother's words, the hidden life of the greatest, wisest, meanest of mankind.

None of his great writings have had to come before me, and the comparison of the two different men in him (and alas! in us all as well) brings a feeling of infinite sadness. The two men are distinct as the two sides of a medal! When one is seen the other is invisible, yet both are one.

On the obverse are the noble head, the eloquent features, the speaking eyes. On the reverse not a redeeming feature; drunkenness, debauchery, of the vilest kind according to current reports, gambling, extravagance, forgery, fraud, ingratitude, treachery, and finally the judicial murder of Essex, his patron, to whom he owed all, for the sake of the plunder it might happen to bring. Not a trace of either love or pity for any human being! for his mother inspired only fear; and the desire to be buried in her grave is but the instinct of servitude reasserting itself at the last. Not one act of charity records itself in Bacon's life, even the reference in his diary to the will of "Charterhouse" Sutton relates to the prospective fees which as Solicitor-General he would derive from it.

An aggravated paradox of humanity: inwardly "*concentred all in self*"; outwardly the revealer to Humanity of a new Philosophical Universe—the liberator then and for all time to come of Human Intellect.

But the one closing word must be

MISERERE, REX CÆLORUM
MISERERE MISERORUM.

for, of all that mighty host which has no other help save the Mercy of God, none could stand more in need of it than he.

APPENDIX.

Letters to "The Academy."

LONDON, *April* 13th, 1895.

SHAKESPEARE AND BACON.

LONDON, *March* 23rd, 1895.

THE "Gazetteer" of December 31st, 1766, contains in its last column the following:

"W. wishes some of our critical correspondents would give their opinion of the resemblance between a passage in Shakespeare and one in Anacreon. The passage from Shakespeare reads thus:

"'The sun's a thief, and with his great attraction
Robs the vast sea. The moon's an arrant thief,
And her pale fire she snatches from the sun.
The sea's a thief, whose liquid surge resolves
The moon into salt tears.'—*Timon*, act iv., sc. 7.

"The passage in Anacreon, ode xix., reads:

'πίνει θάλασσα δ' αὔρας
"Ο δ' ἥλιος θάλασσην
τὸν δ' ἥλιον σελήνη.'"

Here our querist stops, and he seems to have got no answer till the Variorum edition of 1803, and Mr. Staunton later on, confirm the resemblance, though the former quotes a version by Ronsard of 1597. No English translation was extant in Shakespeare's time.

This ode of the Pseudo-Anacreon suggests inquiry; and, as a preliminary, I give my own rough version, wherein I sacrifice everything to literalness and metre, condensing even seven lines into six:

> "Deeply drinks the dark-brown field,
> Drinks of it the tree-clad weald,
> Drinks the sun from ocean streams,
> Drink of him the pale moon beams,
> Drinks the sea from showers of sky:
> If they drink, mates, why not I?"

It is a perfect drinking song, and found much favour with roystering classical topers in those drinking days of theirs, which lasted certainly down to Porson's οὔτε τόδε οὔτε τἄλλο.

Now Mr. Halliwell-Phillipps opines ("Outlines," i. 97) that Shakespeare's classical learning was picked up during the period from 1587 to 1592 from the society he kept of Gray's Inn and Temple men, whose masques and pageants he mounted for them. Such a song as Anacreon XIX. must have been in favour at those hard-drinking symposia, at which I have elsewhere established the sodality of Shakespeare[1] and the two Bacons, Francis and Anthony.

Shakespeare's head was strong enough to carry off these carouses; though a later one is said to have killed him; but the two brothers got frightfully upset, as is plain from Lady Ann Bacon's letter to

---

[1] "Middle Temple Table Talk," pp. 50-60.

APPENDIX. 69

Francis of August 20th, 1594 (Spedding's "Life," i. 313):

"Let this letter be unseen. Look very well to your health. Sup not nor sit up late. Surely I think your drinking to bedwards hindreth your and your brother's digestion very much. I never knew any but sickly that used it: besides bad for head and eyes. Observe while yet in time."

We know also from one of Anthony's letters (Spedding, i. 322) that Francis was even then, at thirty-four, troubled with stone.

Here, then, was an opportunity for Shakespeare to pick up the ode which he so magnificently expanded in "Timon."

And may not the intimacy between Shakespeare and Bacon have had other results equally ready to hand? Is it not probable that the money-making actor-manager and "Jack Factotum" would avail himself of the staff of scriveners which Bacon kept for public use at his Twickenham Lodge—especially when we remember the large money transactions for mounting masques, etc., which passed between the two during twenty years (1593-1613)?

No one appears to have noticed that Bacon did keep this scrivener's shop, had many clerks, whom he found it hard work to keep going, and even "sweated" them in his desperate endeavour to extricate himself from his embarrassments. The proof is in a letter from Francis to Anthony Bacon (Spedding, i. 349).

"I have here an idle pen or two, especially one that was cozened, thinking to have got some money this term. I pray send me somewhat else for them to write out, besides your Irish collection, which is almost done.

"There is a collection of Dr. James, of foreign states, largeliest of Flanders, which though it be no great matter, yet I would be glad to have it.—From my lodge at Twickenham, this 25 of Jany., 1594."

Is it going too far to suggest that we may here find the solution of the vexed problems: and perhaps who wrote out, and who kept, the original MSS. of the plays?

A SURVIVAL OF BACON'S TWICKENHAM SCRIVENERY.

LONDON, *April* 10*th*, 1895.

Referring to my letter in the "Academy" of March 30th, in which I evidenced the existence of this hitherto unnoticed phase in Bacon's life, I may be reasonably asked if any book produced there, is still in existence? I shall submit that at least one such has survived, and is in my possession.

I copy its short history from Dr. E. A. Abbott's "Bacon and Essex," p. 165.

In the spring of 1600, after Bacon's temporary reconciliation with Essex, for the purpose of conciliating Essex with the Queen, Francis Bacon, who was supposed to know better than other people what would please the Queen, volunteered to draw up for Essex a letter to Anthony Bacon which Essex might copy out in his own handwriting, and send him; and then Francis would show it to the Queen as a proof of Essex's contrition and loyalty. To make the thing more natural and deceptive, Francis would also dress up in Anthony's name a letter to Essex, which was to elicit in answer the letter abovementioned. The two letters might naturally be supposed to be shown by Anthony to his brother Francis, and Francis might then show them to the Queen."

Essex was much under the influence of Anthony, and Chamberlain writes to Carleton, on June 28th, 1599, that he proposed to give him Essex House.

The letters thus "faked up" were admirable imitations of the several styles of the supposed writers—catching the quaint, humorous, cumbersome language of Anthony, as also the abrupt, incisive, and passionately rhetorical phrasing of the Earl (Abbott, p. 185). It is our first instance of Bacon's writing in the name and style of other people.

Both Essex on his trial and Bacon in his "Apology" (Abbot, App., p. 17) allege all these facts; and the passages need not be quoted, except for one important sentence to be alluded to later on.

The title of our pamphlet is, "To Maister Anthonie Bacon, An Apologie of the Earle of Essex against those which falsely and maliciously taxe him to be the only hinderer of the Peace and quiet."

My copy is post octavo, of about 100 pp., and contains five documents: (1) The Apologie, dated at foot, April 8, 1600. (2) Reasons for the peace with Spain in 1598. (3) Reasons against the peace with Spain in 1598, dated at foot, April 15, 1600. (4) A morning prayer agreeable to the Lord's Prayer. (5) A prayer at night going to bed. (6) A prayer for the Sabaoth.

The book is beautifully written, "without a blot," and is clearly contemporary with the inception of the idea, when Essex had been a close prisoner for eight months, and was to continue so for three more. It contains the first of the "Apologie," a document addressed to the future; two out-of-date historical documents which had lost their interest save to Essex alone, and for which he would have an author's affection; and three prayers suited for a man who had been perilously near the gates of death, and was in great temporal distress as well. In fact, Bacon, in his own "Apology," casts up against Essex his "carrying on a show of religion" —a weakness, by the way, to which Bacon did not yield.

Can this book have been written for any one but Essex's own use, and to his order? It contains his hope for the future, his memories of a brilliant past, his consolation for the present hour of sickness and disgrace; and it is contemporary with the scheme for his restoration to the Queen's favour.

The book had subsequently public interest. Five transcripts, mixed up with other miscellaneous documents up to as late as 1616, exist in the British Museum—one of them in French. There is another in the Record Office, not dated; two (of the "Apologie" alone) were in the recent Phillipps' sale—that which belonged first to Sir Julius Cæsar, and afterwards to Horace Walpole (4to size), fetched £5 10s. My own seems to have been annotated by Dr. Grosart; and one would like to know if the Bodleian and other great libraries have not also copies, and whether they contain any documents personal to Essex.¹ If not, I submit that my pamphlet is an early copy written for, and by order of, the unhappy favourite of Elizabeth.

Mr. Saunders (law stationer in Portugal Street) has no doubt the pamphlet was written by a professional scrivener. The British Museum and Record Office have nothing to say against this— they say it is vastly superior to the handwriting of the time. The book has been shown to Sir E. Maunde Thompson, K.C.B.; Mr. Maxwell Lyte, C.B., who corrected the date of the Record Office Transcript to the date of this; and Mr. Scott, head of the MSS. Department, British Museum. It has been exhibited at the Library of the Royal Institution, Middle and Inner Temples and Gray's Inn. No corrections or contradictions have appeared, although I was told many had sat down for the purpose, but found "something staggering about it."

But how do we connect it with the newly discovered Twickenham copying shop? Firstly, the date is contemporaneous with an idea admittedly originated and secretly carried out by Bacon; it was a State document, and he would not have it "faired out" anywhere else. Secondly, a slip in Bacon's own "Apology" (quoted by Abbott, App., p. 17) shows that he kept control over its issue. The passage runs: "which letters [*i.e.*, Anthony to

¹ This query has produced no reply.

Essex and this " Apologie "] cannot now be retracted or altered by reason of my brother *or* his lordship's servants' *delivery* long since comen into other hands."

A liar's evidence is good against himself. Anthony and Essex were in this matter mere puppets of Francis from the very first, and the " delivery " or putting into circulation, which he himself speaks of, would be under his own control. Till the Queen had seen it, no issue, save this to Essex himself, would be permissible; and we know the Queen did not receive it until she dined with him in the summer at Twickenham, when he tells us, with an author's whimsical vanity, that he presented her with a sonnet which was commended by those who saw it. The poet Bacon!

May I somewhat expand the reasons why Shakespeare should employ the Twickenham Scrivenery for his MSS. and theatre copying?

In 1596 Bacon was absolutely shackled with debt on all sides. He had " rooked " (there is no other word for it) his cousin Robert Bacon into making over to him £600 a year, on the assurance that he would stand Robert's friend with the Lord-Keeper in a suit to which Robert was a party—Francis never did anything of the kind, as Robert piteously bewails. He had ruined his creditor Trott, as that victim complained to Anthony with tearful eyes. He had stripped Anthony of everything, so that he had to contemplate alienating

Gorhambury. He pestered everybody (save his mother) for loans.

Would he not apply to Shakespeare? Could the manager refuse the Master of Gray's Inn Revels, when there were four other theatre companies ready to step into his shoes? Moreover, Shakespeare was flush of cash, and had to employ other capitalists, in order to put out his spare money.

Shakespeare's difficulty was, "How am I to get it back from Bacon?" He was a keen man of business, and sued at least three of his debtors, and their sureties; he was not afraid of looking after his money, even from a fellow-townsman. His only way was to "take it out in work" at Twickenham, and he may even have suggested to Bacon an idea so foreign to all that Queen's Counsel's experience.

Twickenham would provide Shakespeare with the amanuensis to write down the plays from his dictation, would copy out the MSS. themselves, and the actors' and prompters' parts without a blot—as Heminge and Condell tell us; would have them all in order for reference or copying at the moment, and the cost would be put down to "my account with you."

I must leave others now to examine the documents which I have carefully collected, searched, and studied for many years, in the hope that some lost passages of Elizabethan times may thus be brought to light.

"*Si quid novisti rectius istis candidus imperti si non utere his mecum.*"

N.B.—It is only fair to say that these questions have not as yet met with a reply.

INDEX.

Allen. Corruptness of Elizabeth's Court, 9.

"Apologie," The. Original cause of quarrel between Elizabeth and Essex, 51.

—— also of his disgrace and death, 53.

—— my copy made by the Bacons at the Scrivenery, April 8th, 1600, for Essex's private use, 51.

—— first written by Essex at sea, when returning from the Spanish expedition, and sent through his secretary, Cuffe, to Anthony, for translation and circulation on the continent under a false name, 46.

—— Elizabeth threatens Cuffe with death if it is printed, 46. (N.B.—A threat ultimately carried out.)

—— Anthony transcribes it nevertheless, 52.

—— French translation by Fontaine (Minister of the French Church in London), Dutch by Sir Thomas Bodley, Spanish by Standen, 52.

—— Spaniards, greatly angered, attribute it to Anthony, 52.

—— Francis prints 200 copies to anger the Queen and bring about Essex's ruin, 56.

—— Elizabeth furious, imprisons two persons, and orders all copies to be got in, 56.

—— Essex writes Stationers' Company (which has no record of it) and Archbishop of Canterbury to same effect, 56-7.

—— all copies got in during May, 1600, 56-7.

—— Essex writes Elizabeth that the Bacons had printed it to *ruin* him, "they will also play him on the stage, which is 1,000 times worse than death," 57.

—— Francis admits having circulated it through Anthony's and Essex's servants, 74.

—— sharp spar about it between Francis and Essex on the latter's trial, 74.

"Apologie," The. Bacon's admission about it in his own "Apology," published after Essex's execution, 71.
—— printed, much circulated, and popular after Essex's death, 72.

Bacon, Lady Ann. Her power over her sons, 16.
—— her close watch upon them, 16.
—— her complaint of Francis's gambling, 1593, 16.
—— her complaint of the drunkenness of both her sons, 17.
—— her termagant temper, 16, 17.
—— her spending all her substance upon her sons, 17.
—— her letter reproving Essex for adultery, his meek denial, 31.
—— her horror of stage plays, 32.
—— her protest against Gray's Inn Revels, 1594, 33.
—— how it came to pass that the screw came quickly to act on her sons, 33.
—— the Revels modified: Francis's name and authorship kept out of sight for a century, 34.
—— her influence debars Francis from any avowed connection with the stage till her death in 1610, 36.

Bacon, Anthony. Foreign correspondent for many years on the continent for Burleigh, 40.
—— returns to England, 1572, in ill health, 40.
—— coldly received by the Cecils, and not employed by them in Government work, 40.
—— being greatly in debt, sets up a public scrivenery, where he transcribes for sale MSS. he collects from England and the continent, 41.
—— names of some of the authors, 42.
—— introduced to Lord Essex by Francis, 15, 40.
—— becomes his private secretary at £1,000 a year salary (£7,000 now), 15.
—— transfers the Scrivenery to Essex's service for foreign correspondence, 15.
    its enormous expense, 43.
—— to escape from the monopoly of the London Scriveners' Company, transfers it to Twickenham Park, a house of Lord Essex's, but occupied by the two Bacons, which he afterwards gives to Francis, 41.

Bacon, Anthony. Enlists all his old correspondents so as to enable Essex to supply the Queen with earlier foreign information than Burleigh, 42.
—— engages others as decipherers and translators. Phelipes (Walsingham's decipherer), Standen, Sir Thomas Bodley, Fontaine, Guicciardini—forty or more, 42.
—— deciphering done only at Twickenham, 42.
—— the cipher kept back from Essex, 42.
—— Standen, sketch of his life, 42.
—— thinks of selling Gorhambury, 53.
—— plot and counter-plots in Scotland. The Edinburgh correspondents, 43.
—— bribed by Foulis there, 43.
—— in January, 1600, Anthony threatens Essex, when ill, with the discovery of above to Cecil, 54.
—— Essex buys his silence by the gift of all the property he had left: Essex's house in the Strand, value £2,000 then, £14,000 now, 54.
—— the Queen, indignant at the transaction, compels Anthony to quit the house after Essex's execution, and the family redeem the house for £4,000. What did Anthony do with the money? he died penniless. 58.
—— work done at the Scrivenery for Bacon's private profit, 44, 45.
—— work falling short, Francis writes Anthony to hunt up more work, 45.
—— Essex returning from Spain, sends him by his secretary Cuffe draft of "Apologie"—he is to have it translated by Fontaine, and circulated on the continent anonymously or under false name, 45.
—— N.B.—Anthony great at anonymous letters and writing Lady Northumberland, Essex's sister, one as to her husband's adultery, 46.
—— Elizabeth threatens Cuffe with death if it is published (a threat she ultimately carries out); nevertheless, Anthony transcribes and scatters it broadcast, 46.
—— it forms three long, closely written sheets, 46.
—— Petit, government spy at Liège, reports to Cecil the anger of the Spaniards at Anthony's pamphlet, adding

that he *makes comedies of their king on the stage*, 52.

Bacon, Anthony. At Essex's desire, when ill in April, 1600, makes copy of " Apologie " for his use, adding certain prayers, which copy is now in my hands, 55.

— to incense Elizabeth against Essex, prints 200 copies of "Apologie;" added Lady Rich's offensive letter as greater aggravation. (*Vide* Sydney Papers.) After Essex's execution the Queen compels him to leave Essex's house. 56.

— destroys the bulk of his later papers, 61.

— dies of remorse within four months after Essex's death in debt and disgrace, 58.

— his death only recorded by Chamberlain as bringing no benefit to Francis; so that the Essex House money had vanished. Where had it gone to? Probably handed to Francis, who gambled it away or spent it on another jewel. 58.

Bacon, Francis. Reproved by his mother for gambling, 16.

— — Reproved by his mother for drunkenness also, 17.

— his mother protests against Gray's Inn Revels, December, 1594, 17-33.

— how it happened that the screw worked so quickly, 33.

— heavily in debt to Essex and others, 33, 41.

— introduces Anthony to Essex as private secretary, 41.

— his money straits, 33.

— Essex gives him Twickenham Park, worth £2.000 (£14,000 now), for which sum he afterwards mortgages it, 15, 41.

directs Anthony to hunt up " copy " for the Scrivenery, work being short, 45.

arrested for a debt of £300, 33.

his extravagance and rapacity, 44.

acts as broker for prisoners' pardons with the Court ladies, to whom the Lord Chancellor has assigned the sale, 9.

— acts generally as a professional director of pageants, 35.

— Master of Gray's Inn Revels, 1589-1614. Employs Lord Chamberlain's players all the time, 13.

INDEX. 81

Bacon, Francis. Composes six speeches in the "Masque of Flowers," 1594, 28.

—— N.B.—Campion only claims one of the songs in it. Who wrote the others? 29.

—— the Play of "Errors," 35.

—— intimate with Shakespeare from 1588, and with Ben Jonson also, 13, 38.

—— intimate also with Lord Chamberlain's players, to whom "Gray's Inn much bounden," 38.

—— "Contrives," the pageant at Palatine's wedding, performed by them, 37.

—— prosecutes Essex the first time, 14.

—— apologizes and is forgiven, 14.

—— in March, 1600, writes the Queen that his brother must sell Gorhambury, and that his creditors insult him. Asks for land worth £80 a year (perhaps £1,000 then). Elizabeth refuses. 53.

—— in his despair, decides to obtain money by Essex's death and forfeiture, 54.

—— as the "Apologie" was a sore point with Elizabeth, decides to print it, appending to it an intemperate letter from Lady Rich (Essex's sister) to the Queen, for writing which she had been twice had up before the Privy Council. Issues 200 copies. 56.

—— Elizabeth furious, imprisons two men and orders the book to be seized, which was effected during May, 56.

—— Essex writes the Queen that the printing was the work of the Bacons, who could *also play him on the stage*, 56.

—— does this and Petit's letter show Bacon to have had the control of a theatre? 57.

—— Bacon acknowledges his publication of the "Apologie" on Essex's trial, and in his own subsequent "Apology," therefor Bacon prosecutes Essex to the death, 57.

—— from the fines and forfeitures of Essex's convicted adherents obtains £1,200 out of Catesby's fine, 58.

—— puts off Hickes, a creditor who applies for some part of it, for four months, 58.

G

Bacon, Francis. Shakespeare receives £700 from some quarter, which he lays out in the Combe lands. Halliwell cannot guess where it comes from. Can it be out of Catesby's fine and from Bacon? No other channel seems possible. 58.

—— could Bacon have been Shakespeare's protector against prosecution for the deer-stealing felony? He prosecuted for such an offence an Attorney-General so late as 1614, and was practically Government General Prosecutor from 1592 downwards. Could the fear of such prosecution be the cause of Shakespeare "lying low" all his London life—herein differing from all his fellow actors and managers, who ruffled it bravely? Could Shakespeare, in view of this and Bacon's power of giving employment as Manager of Gray's Inn Revels, refuse to lend him money? for which Bacon worried everybody else, without exception. Would not the Scrivenery be availed of to repay him by copying his theatre work, setting one debt against another? 23.

—— did Bacon write the Epitaph prefixed to Second Folio? 59.

—— Why it was omitted from the First Folio, 65-73.

Bodley, Sir Thomas. English ambassador in Holland, afterwards founder of Bodleian Library. Acts as foreign correspondent of Anthony Bacon. 43.

—— Translates the "Apology" into Dutch, 46.

—— Acquires the Bishop of Faro's Library as a gift from Essex, and adds it to what is now the Bodleian at Oxford, 7.

Bridges, Mrs. A maid of honour too intimate with Essex. Elizabeth drives her from Court with oaths and blows. 8, 32, 53.

Burleigh, Lord. From his dislike of Francis Bacon's "vanities," otherwise follies and vices, will not employ him in the Public Service, 12.

Campian. Claims one song only in "The Masque of Flowers," 29.

Carre. Bacon's letter to him about the pageant he (Bacon) would get up for his marriage—reveals a great deal, 38.

INDEX. 83

Chamberlain's Company of Players. Employed by Bacon, 1591-1614, 13.
Chamberlain Letters. Confirm Essex's blackmailing by Anthony, 43, 56.
—— the printing of the " Apologie," 56.
—— Bacon chief contriver of the " Palatine's Mask," 49.
—— Essex's ill health in the spring of 1600, 55.
—— Anthony Bacon's death in poverty, 58.
" Comentarius Solutus." Bacon's private note-book, 1608, 48.
Court Ladies sell pardons. Bacon and Standen act as brokers between them and the prisoners, 9.
Crockford. His rise by the turf held no disgrace. Duke of Wellington asks to be member of Crocky's, 19, 20.
Cryptograms. A false issue, 2.
Cutting Cards by one of Nelson's captains for £90,000 at Brooke's Club, 21.

Dorset Estate. Bacon cadging through a servant for the scrivenery work thereof in 1608. Record thereof in his private diary. 48.

Edinburgh Correspondents of Anthony Bacon. Plot and counter-plot. Sir Henry Foulis bribes Anthony himself in the Scotch interest. Anthony blackmails Essex thereon—obtains all the property the Earl had left, namely, Essex House, Strand, for his silence. 43.
Elizabeth. Corruptness of her Court, her passion for and jealousy of Essex, 8.
Essex, Lord. His arms engraved on the spot where he scaled the walls of Cadiz, 14.
—— his average income £32,000 a year—£210,000 now, 44.
—— rebuked by Lady Ann Bacon for adultery. His meek reply. 31.
—— sends Anthony the "Apologie" for translation and foreign circulation under a false name, 45.
    A copy, with the addition of certain suitable prayers, made 8th April, 1600, at the Scrivenery for his own private use, now in my possession.
—— the cipher at Scrivenery kept back from him, 42.

INDEX.

Essex, Lord. Francis Bacon's influence over him. *Vide* Mr. Lee's statement in "Dictionary of National Biography," "Essex." 14.
—— blackmailed by Anthony into giving him Essex House, House, Strand, value £2,000 then, 43, 54.
—— redeemed by the family for £4,000, which amount gulfed in Anthony's debts, as he died penniless, 54.
—— having taken, as his share of the plunder of Faro, the bishop's library, gives it to Sir Thomas Bodley as a nucleus of the Bodleian, 7.
—— committed to custody in his own house, 53.
—— his monopoly of sweet wines withdrawn, 53.
—— after the Bacons have printed the "Apologie," reveals to the Queen their connections with the stage, and their power to "*play him upon it*," 56, 57.

Faunt (Walsingham's secretary). Corruptness of Elizabeth's Court, 9.
Fontaine (Minister of the French Church, London), translator for the Scrivenery, turns the "Apologie" into French, 46.
Foulis (agent of King James at Edinburgh) bribes Anthony Bacon, in the Scotch interest, against Essex, 43.

Gambling universal among all classes, 9.
—— cause of the Bacons' ruin and of Shakespeare's rise, 11.
—— gambling terms rarely mentioned by Shakespeare, 26.
—— disapproved of in "Hamlet," 26.
—— Gray's Inn Masque, 1594; splendid affair. Bacon writes six speeches in it. 35.
—— their play must be classical, and translated by one of their own members, 28.

Harrington, Sir John (courtier and Elizabeth's godson). His character, by Bishop Creighton, 22.
—— a frequent resident at Combe Abbey, his cousin's house, near Coventry, 24.
—— a writer on gambling, gives a list of games, 22.

Harrington, Sir John. His positive evidence as to Shakespeare's supporting his hungry family, and buying New Place by money from that source, 22, 23.

Hope, Mrs. " Diamond," a terrible termagant. She frightens a very tough solicitor, 34.

James, Dr. (chaplain to Lord Leicester). Some of his works wanted for "copy" by Bacon, to write out at the Scrivenery, 45.

Liège Spy. His account of the "Apologie," which he states is written and circulated by Anthony Bacon in 1599. It contains three long sheets, 56.

Marlow, Landlady at, chucks out big bargee, 34.
Middle Temple Hall, Gambling in, 10.
—— benchers refuse me access to documents relating to the production of "Twelfth Night" there, 36.
Mumchance. A costermonger's game, 26.

Northbrooke, Gambling alluded to by, 10.
Northumberland, Lady (Essex's sister). Anthony writes her an anonymous letter about her husband's adultery, 1577, 46.

Oxford Man. His reason for not attending Morning Chapel, 16.

Palatine's Wedding. Bacon "contrives" the masque which Lord Chamberlain's players perform, 37.
Palmer (correspondent for Burleigh at St. Luz). Engaged for Scrivenery by Anthony, 41.
Petit (English Government correspondent at Liège) tells Cecil Anthony Bacon had printed the "Apologie," and that the Spaniards were indignant at his *playing their king in comedies on the stage*, 52.

Rich, Lady (Essex's sister), writes to the Queen an intemperate letter, pleading for her brother. Queen furious.

Lady Rich summoned twice before Privy Council for it, and threatened with a third, 55.

Rich, Lady. Bacon, when printing the "Apologie," prints this letter therewith, 56.

—— 200 copies sent out. The Queen commands all to be got in, which was accomplished in May. Recorded in Chamberlain's letter, 56.

Russell, Mrs., Lady of Honour, 53.

—— Elizabeth jealous of her and Essex: drives her from Court with oaths and blows, 55.

Scrivenery. Set up by Anthony in 1592, probably at Gray's Inn, 41.

—— his foreign correspondence scribed there, as also MSS. for Public Sale: among the authors, Standen, Colman, Faunt, Sir Thomas Bodley, Palmer of St. Luz, 42.

—— when Anthony becomes Essex's private secretary, the Scrivenery goes with him, 41.

—— removed to Twickenham Park, out of reach of City Scriveners' Company monopoly, 41.

—— transcribers, translators, and decipherers engaged, among them Phelipes, Walsingham's decipherer, 42.

—— its enormous expense, 43.

—— cipher kept back from Essex, 42.

—— work being short, and Anthony's Irish collection nearly finished, Francis writes Anthony to hunt up work, especially Dr. James' Flanders collections, 45.

—— Essex sends the "Apologie" to be copied, translated, and circulated abroad anonymously, or under false name, 46.

—— Fontaine translates it into French, Sir Thomas Bodley into Dutch, Standen into Spanish, 46.

—— it comprises three long written sheets, 46.

—— this document the original cause of Essex's quarrel with the Queen, and downfall, 52.

—— Petit (English Government Agent at Liège) ascribes it to Anthony, and says Spaniards are very indignant at the insults to their king, 52.

—— Francis borrows a petition from Topcliffe, which, without permission, he sends to Anthony as worth copying for sale, 47.

Scrivenery. April 8, 1600. Copy of the "Apologie"—now in my possession—with certain prayers added, copied for Essex's private use in his illness, 55.

—— the "Apologie," with Lady Rich's letter, printed there to prejudice Essex with the Queen. 200 copies (see "Chamberlain Letters," efforts to recall the copies), 56.

—— still existing in 1608, as Bacon touts, through a servant, for the Dorset estate copying work. The Theatre work still being done there, 48.

Shakespeare. Personal and family history ransacked; but no attempt made to compare it with Bacon's, although he was closely and necessarily intimate with Bacon as Master of Gray's Inn Revels, 3.

—— who employed the Chamberlain's Players, 1591-1614, 4.

—— and was much bounden to them, 38.

—— deer-stealing, a felony punishable in the Star Chamber. Bacon prosecuting for it in 1614. Can Bacon have shielded him from government prosecution? He had the power to do so, 23.

—— can his constant liability thereto have been the cause of Shakespeare's "lying low" in London? None of the other actors of his rank did so, but ruffled it bravely, 23.

—— does not visit Stratford for *ten* years—till his son's funeral, 23.

—— Shakespeare's position 1586-91, 18.

—— all biographers silent thereon, 18.

—— how does he maintain his "hungry famylee" the while? 18.

—— gambling the only explanation, 18, 20.

—— thought no disgrace in those days, or Greene would have cast it up to him, 21.

—— parallels of Crockford and Swindell in our own time, 19-20.

—— parallels of Georgiana, Duchess of Devonshire, and other Court ladies, 20.

INDEX.

—— Harrington, Sir John. Elizabeth's godson, 22.
—— his character by present Bishop of London, in "Dictionary of National Biography;" often resident with his cousin at Combe Abbey, Coventry, 24.
—— acquainted with gambling, 24.
—— records in his epigrams; list of games then in vogue, 22.
—— gives positive evidence as to Shakespeare's carrying on gambling, both with rich and poor, *as a trade;* and buying New Place with money derived therefrom, 22.
—— example: "The ruin of infant young gentlemen maintains his hungry famylee," 23.
—— Harrington's reason for thus recording it; namely, the local jealousy of the gentry when Shakespeare bought New Place, 24.
—— a man not to be spoken lightly of, and quickly resenting it, 24.
—— hardly ever alludes to gambling in the Plays. Even denounces it three times in Hamlet, 25.
—— Halliwell's question.—"Where did the money come from to buy the Combe lands?" Answered.—It came out of £1,200 (part of 4,000 marks, Catesby's fine), practically Essex's blood-money, given to Bacon as his share thereof, 58.
—— keen man of business, dare not refuse to lend money to Bacon, who was his employer for twenty-one years, and protector against prosecution for the deer-stealing, 50.
—— got repaid by having his theatre work copied at Scrivenery, and crediting Bacon with the cost, 50.
—— did Bacon write Shakespeare's epitaph prefixed to the Second Folio? 59.
—— why it was not inserted in the First Folio, 65.
—— quotes Anacreon in Timon. Did he know Greek? 63.
Standen—the spy on both sides. His life, 9, 42, 46.
Sydney papers describe the printing of the "Apologie," 56.
Swindell. His rise by the turf, 19.

Tray trip. Costermonger's gambling game—the three the winning card, 26.

Topcliffe. His M.S. petition borrowed by Bacon for two or three days; and as a document likely to sell, ordered by him without Topcliffe's consent to be copied quickly at the Scrivenery, 47.

Wolfe, General, and Gray's "Elegy," 1.
Whitehall. The same scaffold used at Prince of Orange's wedding, and at execution of Charles I., 37.
—— print of it in my possession, dated 1649, shows that the north window was not used for the king's entry, but the middle one, 40.
Wotton, Sir Henry, one of Essex's four secretaries, confirms the blackmailing of Essex by Anthony, corroborated by Chamberlain, 43-54.

www.ingramcontent.com/pod-product-compliance
Lightning Source LLC
Chambersburg PA
CBHW020140170426
43199CB000I0B/819